So Send I You

"Floyd McElveen raises a clarion call to evangelism in this book, "So Send I You," (previously "Unashamed"). I agree that the church needs to get back to soul-winning as our highest calling. Mac evaluates the problems, eliminates the excuses and motivates our hearts to reach the world for Christ. Get this book and share it with a friend."

•••The late Jerry Falwell, founder and ex-chancellor, Liberty University, Lynchburg, Virginia

"I can think of few people more eligible to write a book on soul-winning. For as long as I have known him, Floyd McElveen has faithfully obeyed our Lord's command to share the gospel wherever we go. This is a wonderful book (previously "Unashamed") for those who want to witness but are not sure how to go about it."

•••Dr. John Ankerberg, president, Ankerberg Theological Research Institute and host, THE JOHN ANKERBERG SHOW

"Winsome—and extraordinarily productive! Witness Floyd McElveen will stimulate us all to seriously reconsider our stance toward the lost—and to do something about it!"

•••Marshall Macaluso, Mission to the Americas

"We have the privilege and the mandate to take the Good News of salvation to those in desperate need of rescuing. The Savior has given us His indwelling Spirit and power to do so. Pastor McElveen displays his pastor's heart for the lost and for Christians who miss out on this great blessing. God's Word is the key. With it we can be bold and bear fruit which lasts for eternity."

•••John Morris, president, Institute for Creation Research

So Send I You

A burning passion to share Christ

Floyd C. McElveen

Big Mac Publishers, Riverside, Ca 92504 WWW.BigMacPublishers.com

Previous ISBN: 1-59052-271-0

Current ISBN-13: 978-0-9823554-3-5

Author:	Floyd C. McElveen
Editor:	Greg Bilbo
Cover photo © 2009:	Mike Hockett
Cover Illustration / Design:	Greg Bilbo

Unless otherwise indicated, Scripture quotations are from:
The Holy Bible, New King James Version © 1984 by Thomas Nelson, Inc.
Other Scripture quotations are from:
The Holy Bible, New International Version (NIV) © 1973, 1984 by International Bible Society, used by permission of Zondervan Publishing House
New American Standard Bible (NASB) © 1960, 1977, Lockman Foundation
The Holy Bible, King James Version (KJV)

Library of Congress Control Number: 2009930709
Library of Congress subject headings:
1. REL030000 RELIGION / Christian Ministry / Evangelism
2. REL045000 RELIGION / Christian Ministry / Missions
3. REL080000 RELIGION / Christian Ministry / Preaching

BIASC / BASIC Classification Suggestions:
1. Evangelism (Christian theology)
2. Evangelism for laymen.
3. Evangelism -- United States -- Controversial literature.

ISBN-13: 978-0-9823554-3-5
ISBN-10: 0-9823554-3-2
1.0

Published by Big Mac Publishers
www.bigmacpublishers.com / Riverside, California 92504
Printed and bound in the United States of America

Acknowledgements

Nothing works unless God is in it and the Holy Spirit uses it to His glory. With my son Greg's hard work and editing, this book, "So Send I You" (previously "Unashamed") was republished. Recently "Faith Of An Atheist" was also published.

My whole family, my wife Virginia, sons Greg, Rocky and Randy, and daughter Ginger, have been an encouragement and help in my writing career for Christ, and we know many have been saved.

Rocky owns a hunting/fishing lodge in Alaska, and speaks all over America during the few months he spends back in California. He has spoken a number of times for Focus on the Family, and other groups. He is used by churches to speak nationwide, and has had as many as 2,500 men out to a recent meeting, with many decisions for Christ.

He wrote a book, which is very popular, "Wild Men, Wild Alaska," and has just released another book, "Wild Men, Wild Alaska II" that should be just as popular.

In His abundant Love,

Bro. "Mac" (Rev. Floyd C. McElveen)

Dedication

I am happy to dedicate this book to my beautiful wife of 60 years, Virginia McElveen, who for the first time in all the books I've written, lovingly wrote a chapter for me in another book, "Faith Of An Atheist," titled "Mr., Where Does This Train Go?"

I also dedicate this book to Richard Hughes who helped me financially with the publishing expenses to get the book republished.

Floyd C. McElveen

Table of Contents

Introduction

Every Christian Can Be a Soul Winner

When I say to the wicked, "O wicked man, you shall surely die!" and you do not speak to warn the wicked from his way, that wicked man shall die in his iniquity; but his blood I will require at your hand.
Ezekiel 33:8

He who continually goes forth weeping, bearing seed for sowing, shall doubtless come again with rejoicing, bringing his sheaves with him.
Psalm 126:6

"Follow Me, and I will make you fishers of men."
Matthew 4:19

"From now on you will catch men."
Luke 5:10

"For the Son of Man has come to seek and to save that which was lost."
Luke 19:10

"As the Father has sent Me, I also send you."
John 20:21

A House in Flames

Chapter One

Rescue those being led away to death;
hold back those staggering toward slaughter.
If you say, "But we knew nothing about this,"
does not he who weighs the heart perceive it?
Does not he who guards your life know it?
Will he not repay each person
according to what he has done?

Proverbs 24:11–12

It's a beautiful Saturday afternoon in midsummer. And what could make the day any better? It's your wedding anniversary.

Bob and Anna, old and dear friends, have offered to come over and watch your kids so that you and your spouse can spend some time alone. After a leisurely afternoon of window-shopping and an early dinner at an outdoor cafe, you stroll home hand in hand through the rosy twilight.

Suddenly you smell smoke.

Quickening your steps, you turn the corner onto your own street. To your horror, you see a house in flames! Even as you begin to run, you know with sickening certainty that it's your home.

"The children!" you both cry, breaking into a head-long sprint. But of course, you tell yourselves, your friends will have gotten them out to safety . . .

Just then, above the roar of the flames, you hear the terrified screams of children trapped by the fire. Running full tilt, you stumble into two spectators halfway down the street. Bob and Anna, the friends you had trustingly left to look after your kids, are leaning casually against a bus shelter, watching the house burn and listening to the piercing screams.

Anna says, "Hi there. Say, what do you think of your lawn? Bob spent most of the afternoon mowing it. Nice job, huh?"

Bob chimes in. "And take a look at the flowerbeds. Anna weeded all of them—even deadheaded the petunias."

You stare at your friends in stunned disbelief as, before your eyes, your house collapses with a roar into a blazing inferno. At that moment, the shrieks of your children are cut off.

It's too late. They're gone.

"Murderers!" you want to howl at the people you thought were your friends. "Dear God! Bob, Anna, what's wrong with you? Our son—our daughter—why didn't you save them?"

Brokenhearted, hopeless, you are left staring at the flaming ruins. Too late, you hear sirens in the distance. But there's nothing left. Even if you wanted to, you couldn't see the neat lawn and freshly weeded flowerbeds through your blinding tears. Your "friends" have failed you, and your precious children have needlessly burned to death.

This is a picture of believers who become busy with a thousand lesser things and neglect to share their faith in Jesus Christ.

Histrionic? Melodramatic? Drawn out?

Not if you really believe in the literal reality of Hell—the biblical Hell where those outside of Christ will dwell forever. Not if you believe that multitudes are going there, even though God declared that He is "not willing that any should perish but that all should come to repentance" (II Peter 3:9).

This is a picture of those who die without receiving forgiveness and salvation in Christ. John 3:16 tells us that God loved the world and sent His Son, Jesus, so that whoever believes in Him would not have to perish, but could instead find eternal life. Jesus Himself "is the atoning sacrifice for our sins, and not only for ours but also for the sins of the whole world" (I John 2:2, NIV).

Jesus said, "For the Son of Man has come to seek and to save that which was lost . . . As the Father has sent Me, I also send you" (Luke 19:10; John 20:21).

God sends all Christians to win the lost to Christ.

How can we say we love Jesus, or that we love those out-side of Christ, if like Bob and Anna we put other things—even good things—ahead of that high calling? Jesus declared, "Do you not say, 'There are still four months and then comes the harvest?' Behold, I say to you, lift up your eyes and look at the fields, for they are already white for harvest!" (John 4:35).

God is passionate about this business of drawing men and women to Himself. In the parable of Luke 15:11–32, the father—who represents God—runs to meet his prodigal son.

Now is the time to start.

Winning people to Christ is our priority—at any cost—because it is God's priority.

Multitudes of Christians today are showing God the "lawns" they've mowed, the "flowerbeds" they've clipped for Him, while He weeps for those passing into an eternity of separation from Him. Where is our sense of urgency?

Like Bob and Anna in the story above, Satan has continually used the good to be the enemy of the best. Anything he can do to convince Christians that they might not be responsible for personal evangelism delights him. Historically, when Christ turned the world upside down through the loving witness of the early Christians, Satan developed and nurtured the split between clergy and laity. The laity soon felt that evangelism was the job of the "professionals"—and washed their hands of any responsibility.

Doctrine is indispensable to our faith—so Satan gets believers wrapped up in theological nitpicking while a world perishes. Imagine two lifeguards allowing a swimmer to drown while they argue over which of them has the better swimming technique! Sound doctrine is vital, but we dare not allow arguments over fine points of theology to keep us from the most pressing task at hand: reaching those who need Jesus.

Learning evangelism techniques will be immensely helpful in your witnessing . . . but the key issue isn't this method or that method, this technique or that technique. The key is to begin and to persevere, in the power of the Holy Spirit.

Where Are the Tears?

Through the modern evangelical movement, God began again to awaken His people to the responsibility of every believer to reach out to nonbelievers with the good news of salvation. And again Satan went into action. The results can be seen in much of the current casual approach to soul-winning—sophisticated programs and methodologies, but no heartbroken prayers. And no tears. True repentance or conversion always comes at a cost.

Those who sow in tears shall reap in joy. He who continually goes forth weeping, bearing seed for sowing, shall doubtless come again with rejoicing, bringing his sheaves with him (Psalm 126:5–6).

Go, weep, and sow with the passion of a loving Christ pouring through you, and you will surely rejoice as you bring in the harvest. This is not a promise for an elite few. This is God's will and desire for all believers, no matter what our inclinations or gifting. "The fruit of the righteous is a tree of life, and he who wins souls is wise" (Proverbs 11:30).

Does God want only some Christians to be wise? Obviously not. Did God equip only some Christians to be soul-winners? By no means. Every Christian can win souls, and therefore every Christian should win souls.

In Acts 8:1–4, we find that the apostles (the preachers) were detained in Jerusalem, while the new converts, many of them less than a year old in Christ, were all scattered abroad. They were the ones who "went everywhere preaching the word."

"But," you might say, "God wants some as sowers, and others as reapers." That's true . . . up to a point. Yet if that same philosophy was applied to world missions, we might find ourselves distinguishing and categorizing those who pray, those who give and those who go. And what would that mean? That no one who prays needs to go? That no one who gives needs to pray? That no one who goes needs to pray or give?

That would make no sense at all.

In the passage sometimes used to support the idea that believers are either sowers or reapers (I Corinthians 3:1–7), the apostle Paul makes the point that neither he nor Apollos has anything to boast about, since it is God alone who gives the increase. When Paul states, "I planted, Apollos watered" (v. 6), does that mean he was never a reaper—a soul-winner? Does it mean that Apollos was never a planter, or that Paul never watered? Of course not.

Paul is demonstrating in these verses how he and Apollos complemented each other in their work for Christ. He exposes the folly of carnal division by some Christians who were saying, "I am of Paul" or "I am of Apollos"—as if those men were anything in themselves. It is God who gives life. It is God who brings about the new birth. The Spirit of God acts on the Word of God to give forgiveness and eternal life to those who trust in the blood of Christ and His bodily resurrection—those who believe in and receive Him as their Lord and Savior.

I often reap where others have sown the seed, and others often reap where I have shared the gospel. This passage was never meant to establish unbreakable categories—or provide excuses for those who neither sow nor reap!

I might add that if we sow grain and water grain, it will still rot in the field if we don't reap it! Hear the heart-cry of our Lord and Savior: "The harvest truly is plentiful, but the laborers are few. Therefore pray the Lord of the harvest to send out laborers into His harvest" (Matthew 9:37–38).

God is the ultimate giver of life by His Holy Spirit, but He uses us to sow the seed and reap the harvest.

Jesus said to His disciples, and therefore to us, "Follow Me, and I will make you fishers of men" (Matthew 4:19). How can we claim to be following Christ if we're not fishing for souls?

I heard recently that only about 3 percent of those who profess to be Christians ever lead anyone to Christ! In evangelistic meetings across Alaska, Canada and the Lower Forty-Eight, I have been heartbroken over the response to this simple question: "How many of you have ever led someone to

Jesus Christ?" Often the only responses are from the pastor and his wife, and perhaps a godly deacon or elder.

Even in exceptional churches, where many in the congregation say they have led people to Christ, the real sorrow comes when I ask how many people average leading one individual a year to the Savior. I have spoken in churches with hundreds of members, yet with perhaps a handful of exceptions, I don't recall one in which even twenty or thirty believers could testify to leading one person a year to Christ.

If the early Christians in Jerusalem had cared no more for Jesus and for lost men and women than it seems many congregations do today, the church would never have spread beyond Jerusalem.

What are we doing for the millions now who are lost, and for future generations?

Where would you be if no one had shared the Good News with you? What would have happened to your children?

Some time ago I had to help restrain a ten-year-old girl from plunging into a burning house to try to rescue her dogs. They were trapped in the basement and howling piteously. The flames were real and hot, the cries and moans awful, the tear-streaked face of the little girl heartrending as she sobbed out her love for her pets, struggling all the while as she yearned to rescue them, whatever it cost her.

It broke my heart that this little girl loved her dogs more than we—professing the love of Christ—seem to love the eternal souls of men and women.

Jesus laid it on the line: “If anyone loves Me, he will keep My word” (John 14:23). No waffling. No wiggle room. No ifs, buts, or “maybe when it’s convenient” excuses.

“Do not be afraid,” Jesus said. “From now on you will catch men” (Luke 5:10). When the house is on fire, it’s no time to plant daisies.

Why Win Souls?

Chapter Two

Those who are wise shall shine
Like the brightness of the firmament,
And those who turn many to righteousness
Like the stars forever and ever.

Daniel 12:3

Why Win Souls?

When you're talking about something with consequences in both time and eternity, you could go on listing reasons for the rest of your life. But in the pages of this brief chapter, let me touch on some of the biggest reasons I can think of.

► *Because our Lord and Savior commanded us to.*

"You shall be witnesses to Me in Jerusalem, and in all Judea and Samaria, and to the end of the earth . . . Go therefore and make disciples of all the nations" (Acts 1:8; Matthew 28:19).

If we are born again, He is our Lord—our Boss, our Manager, our Owner. He bought us (I Corinthians 6:20), and we no longer belong to ourselves, but to Him. If He tells us to be His witnesses to the end of the earth, we really have no other option. John warned us about the folly of claiming Him as Lord—and yet ignoring His commands: "He who says, 'I know Him,' and does not keep His commandments, is a liar, and the truth is not in him" (I John 2:4).

► *Because those who die without Christ are eternally lost.*

"There is none righteous, no, not one . . . For all have sinned and fall short of the glory of God" (Romans 3:10, 23).

Years ago, I lost my way deep in the swamps of Mississippi—rattlesnake and water moccasin country. It was just at twilight that I finally began to get my bearings, but I had no flashlight to light my way out. Every step through that dark swamp was torture. I can still feel my heart pounding in my chest as I imagined the dangers lurking in the shadows.

To be lost eternally in Hell is unimaginably worse. The terrors are real, there is no light and there is no way out. Not ever.

►*Because nothing pleases God more.*

No jewel-encrusted earthly crown approaches the supreme value of the crown our Lord holds in store for those who have brought others with them into heaven. No reward is as satisfying as His promise that those who "turn many to righteousness" will shine like "the stars forever and ever" (Daniel 12:3).

►*Because winning souls brings great joy to our lives.*

Many believers seem to just muddle through the Christian life, battling problems, wrestling with perplexities, and wondering what they are missing and where they might find the real joy of salvation. Yet these same Christians would come alive with excitement if they began to consistently share Christ and see people accept Him as Savior. There is no greater thrill for a child of God. And when you have the opportunity to see that individual's life transformed and growing in Christ before your very eyes, that thrill becomes a deep fountain of lasting satisfaction and joy. As Paul said of his spiritual children in Thessalonica, "For what is our hope, or joy, or crown of rejoicing? Is it not even you in the presence of our Lord

Jesus Christ at His coming? For you are our glory and joy" (I Thessalonians 2:19–20).

►*Because winning souls results in changed lives.*

How glorious to see God quiet the hunger of the restless, clarify the confused, rescue and change the alcoholic, the prostitute, the homosexual, the drug addict, the adulterer, and those enmeshed in empty, futile religions. Equally important, He saves us from more subtle sins—envy, jealousy, pride, racism, hate, the fear of death, and the world's hollow and cynical philosophies. He gives the answers to those eternal questions: Where did I come from? Why am I here? Where am I going? He gives hope to the hopeless, love to the lonely, and purpose to the puzzled. Such changed lives have a great impact on society. They are like a city on a hill that cannot be hidden.

►*Because the sacrifice of Christ demands that we win others to Him.*

He hung on that bloody cross, enduring physical, spiritual and emotional torture, forsaken by His friends, His disciples and His Father—for us. Now it's up to us to demonstrate His compassion, love, mercy and grace to a dying, desperate world.

Jesus said, "As long as I am in the world, I am the light of the world" (John 9:5). Now, we who are infused and indwelt with His light are to be lights in that world. "You are the light of the world.... Let your light so shine before men, that they may...glorify your Father in heaven" (Matthew 5:14, 16).

►*Because redeemed individuals bring glory to the Lord.* Think of it! Redeemed men and women, boys and girls bring glory to the risen Savior. If I can glorify Christ by worshiping and serving Him, so can those who come to know Him through my witness. Every blood-bought soul brings honor and glory to the Savior both here and in heaven. "You are worthy, O Lord, to receive glory and honor and power; for You created all things, and by Your will they exist and were created" (Revelation 4:11).

►*Because winning souls demonstrates the power of God.* The world offers its incessant panaceas and platitudes to cure hurting hearts and minds. One answer follows hard upon another—man-made religions, psychological counselors, scientists, philosophers, pills and politics. The intentions may be good, but the results range from temporary euphoria to catastrophic disillusionment. How great a privilege we have to demonstrate the power of God by our changed lives, and the lives of others we reach with the gospel. "For I am not ashamed of the gospel of Christ, for it is the power of God to salvation for everyone who believes" (Romans 1:16).

►*Because winning souls demonstrates the purpose of God.*

When people find salvation in Christ they discover a plan and purpose for their lives beyond anything they'd ever imagined. On top of that, they begin to understand God's plan for the whole scheme of things—the earth, the universe, and the future. That which seemed like a random, heedless hodgepodge begins to make sense. "Because the foolishness of God is wiser than men, and the weakness of God is stronger than men" (I Corinthians 1:25).

►*Because we are grateful.*

Gratitude makes us long to share the love of Christ. If I find something truly lovely, or taste an especially good dish, I can hardly wait to share it with my beautiful wife, Virginia. Sharing Christ says to God over and over again, "Dear Father, I am so grateful for your love, for the salvation you provided through your Son. It is the most wonderful thing that could ever happen to me, and I enjoy sharing it so much."

►*Because of love.*

I love Jesus, and therefore I love my neighbor. It is impossible to separate these two "greatest commandments" on which all the other commandments hang (Matthew 22:37–40; I John 3:14–17; 4:20–21). Can we truly love our non-Christian neighbors if we let them live—and die—without Christ? If the greatest thing that has ever happened to me is salvation through the Lord Jesus Christ, and I am to love my neighbor as myself, I find myself compelled to share Christ with him.

►*Because there is rejoicing in heaven.*

Jesus said, "I say to you that likewise there will be more joy in heaven over one sinner who repents.... There is joy in the presence of the angels of God" (Luke 15:7, 10). How wonderful to know that, by the grace of God and the power of the Holy Spirit working through us, we can bring men and women to Christ to be saved forever, and cause all of heaven to rejoice!

►*Because of the promise of heaven.*

We win souls because of the promise of heaven—a golden city of unimaginable size and shimmering splendor, resting on a foundation of sparkling gems of all colors. In that place, our eyes will drink in a rainbow-encircled throne, golden streets, a crystal river lined with fruit trees, delights unspeakable, and joys incomprehensible. How amazing to think that we can have a part in sharing this sanctuary from sin, sorrow, death and pain with those God allows us to win for Christ. What an experience awaits the redeemed, just a few short years from right now. The music—the worship—the joy—the freedom from all worry, hate, and fear, and the love absorbing all of us in one great family as we serve Him. And in the midst of it all, brighter than a million suns, we will behold the glory of the risen Christ.

► *Because of the reality of Hell.*

Our Lord Jesus Himself, the most loving Person who ever lived, the One who died on the cross for us, said more about Hell than anyone else in the New Testament. Again and again He warned of that awful place.

Scripture makes it clear that this horrible destination is inevitable, inescapable and everlasting for all who have not received salvation in Christ. The same Greek word is used to mean "eternal," as in the eternal God, eternal heaven and eternal Hell. Simply put, if God and heaven are eternal, then Hell is eternal too. Much as we might like to, we cannot pick and choose which parts of God's Word we will choose to believe.

In Luke 16, Jesus tells the story of a rich man and a beggar named Lazarus. The rich man was self-centered and self-indulgent, blind to everything but his own pursuit of pleasure and "the good life." And even though he and his brothers had access to the Scriptures (vv. 28–29), he did not heed them. When he died, he found himself in a place of torment. Lazarus, though a sick outcast begging for crumbs at the rich man's gate, was a believer. When he died he was carried by the angels to his eternal home in heaven.

To me, this passage contains one of the most horrific descriptions in all Scripture, as the rich man begs and pleads for some relief from his torment. "Then he cried and said, 'Father Abraham, have mercy on me, and send Lazarus that he may dip the tip of his finger in water and cool my tongue; for I am tormented in this flame'" (v. 24).

A pastor friend of mine, Paul Schoming, was a volunteer fireman in Anchorage, Alaska. One night he and the other firemen stood helpless as a screaming woman could be seen at the window of her trailer, burning to death. It was awful, pitiful, gut wrenching—but finally it was over. At least that woman's agony had an end.

In Hell, the agony will never end.

James 1:17 tells us, "Every good gift and every perfect gift is from above, and comes down from the Father of lights, with whom there is no variation or shadow of turning." When God is spurned, however, when Jesus is rejected as Lord and Savior, the gifts go back to the Giver. There is not one good thing in Hell, and there never will be.

There is no loving presence of God. No redeeming presence of Jesus. No indwelling presence of the Holy Spirit. Those who did not want God here, will not have Him there.

There will be no love in Hell—because God is love. No sweet embrace. No lover's kiss. No sex. Never the precious softness of a baby in your arms. No comforting word. No hope of change or escape—ever. It is doubtful that anyone will remember you, or know or care that you are there. There is no rest, ever. There is no peace there—only turmoil, eternal panic, and fear. There is no beauty, no majestic mountains, no sparkling lakes, no stately trees, no flowers, no sunset, no sunrise. There is no music—only the cries, screams, curses and groans of lost men and women in total despair and pain. There is no joy. You will never again experience a moment of happiness. Hate fills every atom of Hell.

There is no relief from depression, bitterness, unutterable sorrow, inexpressible grief. No doctor could alleviate the unbearable burning pain and agony that will rack your body and scar your mind as you cry out for a mercy that will never come. No one will take any notice as you scream, "My God, what a fool I was!"

Indeed—there will not be one single moment free of pain in the lake of fire, whether you measure in physical, mental, spiritual or emotional terms. You will grope in darkness and yet burn in flames. One minute will seem like an hour, one hour will seem like a day, one day will seem like a week, one week will seem like months, one month will seem like a year. Like the rich man in Luke 16, you will scream for water. You would give all you ever owned, all the pleasures and treasures you ever had, for one cool drop of water on your tongue, but there is no hope in Hell.

You will be separated from God forever. I fight tears as I write this, but write it I must. Hell is forever!

Is it possible to really love Jesus and let men go to Hell without warning them? I doubt it! How then can we possibly profess to love God and our neighbor, and yet let people go to that unspeakable place—even those who claim they don't care?

When I was in the navy, I knew an eighteen-year-old who managed to get into a Boston nightclub. It was exotic and erotic, a cornucopia of hedonistic pleasures—the decor, the music, the drinking, the laughter. Glasses tinkled; beautiful women danced sinuously in the arms of handsome men.

But suddenly a cry rang out: "Fire! Fire!" Flames and smoke exploded in the crowded club. Panic ensued. Bodies were crushed and trampled as pandemonium reigned. Screams pierced the night, mingled with sobs of fear and despair. My sailor friend was one of the very few to get out. Five hundred people burned to death in that inferno.

No one was sitting around joking that they wanted to be there because that was where their friends were.

Joy, gratitude, changed lives, heaven, Hell . . . when all else is said and done, there remains one great and glorious reason why we should have a burning passion to reach out to men and women who are outside of Christ.

► *Because of Jesus Himself.*

He is the Creator, the King of kings, and Lord of lords. He spoke the universe into being and flung the stars in space, and yet this altogether lovely One died a terrible death for us while we were still sinners. "The Cross" revealed His incredible love for us. "But God demonstrates His own love toward us, in that while we were still sinners, Christ died for us" (Romans 5:8). Jesus came from the palace to the pigpen for us. He endured insults, abandonment, rejection, loneliness, misunderstanding and violent opposition—for us.

He prayed through the long nights—for us. As the Creator (John 1:1–3) as well as the Savior of the world, He feeds us, clothes us, protects us, enables us to take every breath, and monitors every heartbeat—even of those who rail against Him. He wept over blind and rebellious Jerusalem. Knowing full well what lay ahead, He set His face toward the bloody brutality of the cross.

He was so battered and beaten, Isaiah said in prophecy, that "His appearance was marred more than any man" (Isaiah 52:14, NASB).

As He became sin for us, God did not spare His own Son. God the Father was separated from God the Son as Jesus died for us. The soldier's spear thrust into His side caused blood and water to pour out, leading some to say that He died of a broken heart—for us. The blood of Jesus Christ, God's Son, cleanses us from all sin.

And then came the greatest good news this otherwise damned and doomed world could ever hear. As prophets had foretold and Jesus had repeatedly assured His disciples, He rose bodily from the dead. He conquered death and Hell—for us. He is alive, and He is coming again to take those who trust Him as Lord and Savior to be with Him in heaven. He is preparing a place for us. Even now He is with us by His Holy Spirit, promising, "Lo, I am with you always" (Matthew 28:20).

He loves us. Incredible! He loves us!

The most expensive and beautiful mansion in this world would mean nothing to me if I had to live in it without my sweetheart, Virginia. And so it is in heaven for the Lord's redeemed saints. Jesus is what makes heaven a place of incomparable glory and joy.

You will show me the path of life;
In Your presence is fullness of joy;
At Your right hand are pleasures forevermore.

Psalm 16:11

Jesus died in my place. He saved me from sin and Hell. He gave me His gift of everlasting life when I trusted Him. Because of His love, I was born again as His child. He is with me every day. His love surrounds me. He showers His love and grace upon me.

How can I not share Him and His love?

What could possibly be more important in this life?

Let Down Your Nets

Chapter Three

"Launch out into the deep and let down your nets for a catch."

Luke 5:4

Some churches—and even seminaries—teach Christians by word and example that witnessing for Jesus Christ is something of an option.

In other words, it's nice…but not necessary.

"What God really wants," we're told, "is to conform us into the image of His Son. That's what He's all about in our lives, and that's His desire for us."

It's a difficult point to argue.

How could anyone minimize the biblical mandate to be conformed to Christ, to walk in the Spirit, and to grow ever deeper in the spiritual life? Didn't Paul command us to "pray without ceasing" and to "be diligent to present yourself approved to God, a worker who does not need to be ashamed, rightly dividing the word of truth?" (I Thessalonians 5:17; II Timothy 2:15).

As a new Christian, and to this very day, I read the Word every day, seek moment by moment victory through the indwelling power of the Holy Spirit, confess sin as quickly as I recognize it, and serve Him with gladness. All this is the will of God for my life. I have learned to trust Jesus—though how

I wish it were a perfect, imperturbable trust (especially when I have to fly!). I have learned and am learning to navigate by faith, not by feelings, to walk by His grace and not by the law, to strike a balance between legalism and license.

I know His grace is sufficient (II Corinthians 12:9), even though I often feel like I would like to contend with Paul to claim the title "chief of sinners." I have been through the loss of parents as a child, the hell of war and suicide planes, rejection and heartbreak, cold and misery, threats on the Alaskan mission field, and heart attacks. At this very moment, a transplanted heart beats in my chest.

I praise the Lord for what I have learned from many godly writers, leaders and groups about the "deeper spiritual life." They encouraged and uplifted me again and again.

Yet I have seen all too often that, unless personal evangelism is the ultimate reason for their existence, they have missed the mark.

What could be more Christ like than reaching out a hand to a lost soul, leading him to our Lord's glorious forgiveness and salvation? Have we discovered some more spiritual motives, some higher purpose, than the clearly stated motive of the Lord Jesus Christ? (See Luke 19:10.)

Remember the fishing story in Luke 5:1–10? Simon Peter, the expert fisherman, has come ashore and wearily washes his nets after a fruitless night out on the waves. Along comes Jesus and asks Simon to take the boat out again so He can speak to the crowds from the boat. Exhausted and discouraged because he's caught nothing all night, Simon nods his head and does as Jesus requests.

I can just imagine him, once the message is finished, thinking, *Now we can finally go home and catch a little sleep.* Instead, to his utter consternation, Jesus says to him, "Launch out into the deep and let down your nets for a catch" (Luke 5:4).

What is Simon's response? "C'mon, Jesus, You've got to be kidding. You're a good teacher, but I'm the professional and I'm telling You, there's nothing to be caught here. Besides, I've been at it all night, and I can hardly keep my eyes open."

Not quite. The fisherman says, "Master, we have toiled all night and caught nothing." But he doesn't stop there. "Nevertheless," he adds, "at Your word I will let down the net" (v. 5).

Now that is the secret to soul-winning!

1. Go when you feel like it and when you don't.

2. Go by faith and not by feeling.

3. Go when it's convenient and when it's not.

4. Go in season and out of season.

5. Go when you have fished all night and caught nothing.

6. Go when you succeed and when you fail.

Obey God's command: "You shall be witnesses to Me" (Acts 1:8). Never give up, and never give in. Men and women, boys and girls are lost and bound for eternal separation from God. Tell them that Jesus loves them, that He shed His blood for them, and that He died for them.

The Lord commands us to go and declare what we know to be the truth. And He equips us by His Word, and empowers us by His Holy Spirit, to do just that.

Peter obeyed the Lord's command even though he thought it was useless, even though he was tired, even though he didn't feel like it. He trusted the Lord even though he doubted that he would catch any fish. And what was the result of his obedience? They caught so many fish that their nets broke . . . and they filled another boat, belonging to James and John . . . and the boats were so overloaded with the catch that they began to sink.

Jesus then drove home His point to the disciples—and to us. It is not His will that we fish and fish and catch nothing. When we fish for men and women—witnessing in obedience to His command, led by His Word and filled with His Spirit—sooner or later we are going to win souls to Him. We know this, because the Savior Himself said, "Do not be afraid. From now on you will catch men" (Luke 5:10). He does care whether we are successful or not. If we love Him, then we must care too—desperately, urgently, compassionately.

I have been told by good men, leaders, and scholars as well as average Christians, "It's not God's will that everyone necessarily be a soul-winner. Sure, we should witness—but leave the results up to God." Sounds reasonable, even spiritual, doesn't it? And up to a point, I agree. It is God who gives the increase.

But consider Psalm 126:6 again: "He who continually goes forth weeping, bearing seed for sowing, shall doubtless come again with rejoicing, bringing his sheaves with him."

The psalmist isn't talking about wheat farming techniques here. You don't have to weep to have a successful crop of grain. The gospel, however (as with wheat) must be sown—not just known. And "he who continually goes forth weeping" is everyone who sows that seed with the love, compassion, earnestness and tenderness of our Lord Jesus. When that happens, there will be a harvest.

Why weep, if I'm just going to "leave the results up to God?" We are to enter into our Lord's brokenhearted compassion for souls. Of course God gives the results, but we are to care, and care deeply, whether our witness bears fruit or not.

Would you turn on a water faucet and, if nothing came out, just shrug your shoulders and say, "Oh, well, it must be the will of God?" If no water comes out when a faucet is turned on, don't we all try our best to find out why? If I am sharing the water of life, and no lost souls seek to quench their burning thirst, I need to check the flow.

Jesus said—in fact, He stood up and cried out—"He who believes in Me, as the Scripture said, 'From his inner-most being will flow rivers of living water'" (John 7:38, NASB).

Who is drinking of that river of water—the Holy Spirit—flowing through us, so that, like the woman at the well (John 4), they shall never thirst again?

If no water is flowing through us to lost and thirsty souls, why? Are we sure we're connected to the Source—the Savior? Or is something hindering the flow?

If I go fishing and don't catch anything, I need to change my bait, or my location, or do whatever it takes.

I had a dear friend in Alaska, Bill Flynn, whom I was privileged to lead to Christ. Bill fished for a living, and he really knew his business. He had a fine boat, took meticulous care of his equipment, and fished in Bristol Bay, which at that time was a prime location for commercial fishing.

Imagine for a moment that Bill and his wife, Barbara, were desperate for money. Their pantry was low; the mortgage was due. But at last the fishing season was about to begin. Bill left on his hazardous two-month excursion to Bristol Bay. Barbara waited at home. The pile of unpaid bills on the hall table grew thicker every day. The fridge and freezer were empty. Barbara was down to her last few cans of condensed soup. The bill collectors were getting testy.

Finally, Bill came home. With great joy and relief Barbara ran out to embrace her husband. "Thank God!" she cried. "You're safely home!" Now, she tells herself silently, things will be all right. "So," she asks Bill breathlessly, "how big was your catch this year?"

"Barbara, I had the fastest boat in the fleet," Bill tells her. "The sturdiest one, too, for those dangerous waters. And I'm certain I was one of the most skillful and experienced fishermen there. Thank you for helping me repair the net this winter. You should have seen its silvery splendor every time I lowered it into the water. You would have been so proud of me."

"That's wonderful, Bill," Barbara says, somewhat puzzled by his response. "I am proud of you. But how many fish did you get?"

"Well, actually, I didn't catch any fish. But that's not really important, is it? The important thing is that I was out there fishing."

Do you think Barbara would buy that?

Neither will God.

I am not saying there are no other vital aspects to the Christian life than personal evangelism. There is no substitute for loving one another, for daily and intense Bible study, for serious, brokenhearted intercession, for precious times of praise and worship. Nothing can take the place of increasingly intimate fellowship with Jesus as the Holy Spirit applies the Word of God to our hearts, minds, and souls day by day, teaching us to know, love, and obey Him. We need to know biblical doctrine, and stand for God's Word no matter what.

Yet all of these areas of the "deeper spiritual life" should lead us to a deeper desire to seek and save the lost. The only real reason for not reaching men and women for Jesus is a lack of deep love for Him and for the lost. It is a lack of passion for the very reason Jesus shed His blood on the cross, and a lack of obedience to His clear commands. It is a self-centered lifestyle, from which Jesus supposedly saved us. Witnessing to lost souls takes us out of our comfort zone—in the church, at home, and in society.

But it is the most intense and urgent of our Lord's commandments. He said, **"So Send I You"** (John 20:21, KJV).

Will you go?

Will you commit yourself to seeking with all your heart to win souls to your Lord, by His love and grace, for the rest of your life?

The "Gift" of Soul-Winning

Chapter Four

"Peace to you! As the Father has sent Me, I also send you."

John 20:21

Some Christians, I've been told, just don't have the gift of evangelism.

I understand, I think, where they're coming from.

I just don't agree with where they're going.

In Ephesians, Paul writes: "But to each one of us grace was given according to the measure of Christ's gift . . . And He Himself gave some to be apostles, some prophets, some evangelists, and some pastors and teachers, for the equipping of the saints for the work of ministry, for the edifying of the body of Christ" (Ephesians 4:7, 11–12).

New Testament evangelists, in other words, rely on the gifting of the Spirit as much as gifted pastors and teachers. In the first century, some were recognized specifically as "evangelists." In the book of Acts, Paul and his company stayed in the home of Philip, known to all, apparently, as "Philip the evangelist" (Acts 21:8).

And so it is today. There are gifted evangelists in the body of Christ—and it's a wondrous thing to see them in action. They fill big stadiums with massive crowds. They're on television speaking to millions at one time. They can mesmerize an audience, and the Holy Spirit speaks through them in great auditoriums and outdoor meetings and tiny church houses all over the world, bringing conviction and repentance to seekers and skeptics alike. They can wade into a crowd of virtual strangers and begin harvesting left and right for Jesus Christ.

New Testament evangelism seems to include not only soul-winning, but also church planting, discipling, administering, teaching and other unspecified aspects of the spiritual life. It often requires speaking to many people.

There is no doubt about the biblical gift of evangelism. And that's just where the problem lies. We read about this special gifting in Scripture and we say, "Well, that's just not me. That's not my gift. That's not my enabling. That's not my specialty. God has called others to that work, so I really don't need to worry about it or think about it. I'll do my bit in my safe little corner of the kingdom and let others share their faith."

And that is the attitude that is so terribly wrong, and must grieve the heart of God. Don't confuse soul-winning with the broader gift of evangelism.

The truth is, every Christian is commanded and commissioned by God's Word—and by His love—to reach souls for Jesus Christ. Jesus said, "You will be my witnesses" (Acts 1:8, NIV). No one gets a pass on that command. If you are a believer, you are His witness.

We cannot say, "I have the gift of administration (or mercy or giving or faith), but I don't have the gift of sharing my faith. I play the piano, sing in the choir, run the nursery, practice the gift of hospitality, serve as a deacon, teach a class, visit the poor, give to the church, pray a lot, and study my Bible. But since I don't happen to have the gift of soul-winning, I'm not responsible to give my witness for Christ."

Let's look at that thought from a different angle. Suppose you came upon a man who has been shot and is bleeding profusely. His life is fast ebbing away. "Help me!" he begs.

"Oh my," you say. "I am so sorry, sir. I simply don't have the gift of mercy. It's not part of my gifting package. I took a spiritual gifts survey, and mercy was dead last. Just try to hang on, and I'll try to find someone who does have mercy, so he can help you."

What a terrible twisting of Scripture that would be! Yes, there certainly is a gift of mercy (Romans 12:5–8). But that fact doesn't mean that any believer is exempt from showing mercy and demonstrating the love of Jesus. Those especially gifted with mercy, in the sense of these verses, are constantly looking for, sensitive to, and led by God to those who need both normal and exceptional acts of mercy. They especially minister to and lead people to Christ, and encourage other Christians, through exercising their gift. But there is no excuse for any Christian not to help a dying man, whether "gifted" with mercy or not!

In the same way, every Christian—shy or bold, quiet or well-spoken—is still commanded to win souls, just as every

Christian is to show mercy, exercise faith, and give, even though there are those especially gifted in those areas.

The Unadorned Truth

One night in Anchorage, Alaska, I went out witnessing alone to test this belief. Determined not to use any of the soul-winning "techniques" or illustrations I knew, I was armed with nothing but a handful of tracts that presented the gospel through unadorned biblical statements.

I knocked on a trailer door and was invited inside. Two couples were sitting around a table playing cards. I asked them, "May I take a few minutes to show you something wonderful, something life changing?" They agreed, and I simply read, without comment, from the tract, giving each of them a copy so that they could follow along. When I had finished, I asked, with no embellishment whatsoever, if any of them would like to receive Christ as their Lord and Savior. Three of the card players said no. But one of the ladies said yes. There, in front of all the others, she gave her heart and life to the Lord Jesus Christ. Awhile later, when she left Alaska, she contacted me to ask the name of a good church she could join in the town where she was going.

What evangelistic "gift" did I exercise that night?

Any Christian who can read could have done what I did! Even a Christian who can't read would have been able to have them read the booklet out loud and ask them if they wanted to trust Christ. Any Christian can carry a Bible and memorize or point out the verses that deal most directly with salvation. Remember, it is the gospel of Christ—not our words or our presence or our persuasive personality—that is the power of God unto salvation!

Others have told me, "I don't know enough to win souls to Christ. I need to mature more as a Christian; I need to learn how to answer those really tough questions people always ask, before I can be an effective witness."

It's interesting that statistics seem to indicate the very opposite.

It is the new believers—those who have known Jesus for three months, three weeks, or three days—who are the most passionate and effective witnesses for the Savior. The thrill of salvation is so fresh. The Word of God has come alive, and it is electric! They want to learn and apply it for themselves, and to share its riches with their non-Christian friends. They haven't yet retreated into their safe, religious comfort zones. They haven't learned the excuses and lassitude common to so many of us older Christians. Their focus is on Jesus as Savior, and they want others to know Him—no matter what!

This same enthusiasm and joy for outreach should characterize all of us all the days of our life—even as the apostle Paul declared, "For I determined not to know anything among you except Jesus Christ and Him crucified" (I Corinthians 2:2).

After finding the Messiah for himself, Andrew immediately brought his brother Peter to Jesus (John 1:40–42).

And as soon as the woman at the well tasted of the Water of Life, she turned her town in Samaria upside down with her bold witness for the Lord. Imagine! She was the town disgrace; she'd had five husbands and was living with another man. Yet she was so excited that she left her water pot behind and ran into the city, sharing her story with the men there. In spite of what they knew about her sinful life, they listened to her. It must have been immediately obvious that a tremendous change had taken place in this scorned outcast. Her joy at having met the Messiah was contagious. Many of the Samaritans of that city believed on Jesus because of the woman's testimony. Then she led them to Christ in the city, and over the course of two days, many more believed (John 4:1–42).

How long did it take these two people to become powerful soul-winners?

No more than a heartbeat after their conversion!

Theirs was inherently the same mighty testimony as that of the man who had been born blind, whom Jesus healed: "One thing I know: that though I was blind, now I see" (John 9:25).

Almost the moment I found salvation, after I had shared my conversion with my astonished wife, I went as fast as I could to the home of a Mormon elder who had been seeking to convert me to the LDS religion. With tremendous joy I shared with him what Jesus had done for me. I cared little that I couldn't, at that time, counter his carefully orchestrated Mormon arguments. All that mattered was my passion to tell him about my Savior. I wanted to grab him by the lapels. My joy was uncontainable.

That really shook him up.

The elder had been sharing Mormonism with me for some time; I had very nearly been convinced and was ready to be baptized a Mormon. But the very moment I accepted Jesus Christ as Savior and Lord, I saw through the whole charade, and wanted him, my dear friend, to find what I had found.

This chapter is no argument for ignorance, biblical or otherwise. In the many years since I found Christ, I have studied my Bible and grown in Him. I have preached countless Bible messages, written books, and witnessed to hundreds—Mormons included. God has been faithful, blessing these efforts with much fruit through the years. God's Holy Spirit works primarily through His Word, and we need to share it as we grow in knowledge, because "faith comes by hearing, and hearing by the word of God" (Romans 10:17).

Even so, every Christian has a testimony from the moment of salvation.

Never, never, never discount the power of your own story to communicate the love of the risen Christ. All of us can, one way or another, say, "I once was blind, but now I see."

And that, my friend, even that much, is being a witness for Jesus Christ.

Finding Sheep and Feeding Sheep

Chapter Five

"What man of you, having a hundred sheep, if he loses one of them, does not leave the ninety-nine in the wilderness, and go after the one which is lost until he finds it? And when he has found it, he lays it on his shoulders, rejoicing."

Luke 15:4–5

Finding Sheep and Feeding Sheep

Simon, do you love Me?"

The Lord Jesus asked Simon Peter that question three times. And three times He followed it with an unmistakable command: "Feed My sheep."

This is an irrevocable mandate from God to all pastors—and to some extent all believers—to disciple those who have been won to Christ.

But you can't feed sheep that aren't there.

You can't care for a flock of lambs, ewes and rams that don't exist. Until men, women, boys and girls are born into God's family through salvation in Jesus Christ, the sheep corral is empty.

Peter understood that. When He first met Jesus by the sea, the Master commanded him to "catch men." And on the day of Pentecost, after the Holy Spirit had come upon His church in power, Peter "caught" thousands—in one day. Just that quickly, there were multitudes of new sheep to feed and shepherd!

Peter had not entombed himself in his study on that momentous day of Pentecost. He hadn't filled his hours poring over commentaries and comparing translations. He had never been exposed to the idea that pastor-teachers were supposed to limit themselves to preaching the Word, and leave personal evangelism to certain "gifted individuals" in the congregation.

Peter preached with boldness and passion, calling his very nation to "repent and be baptized . . . in the name of Jesus Christ" (Acts 2:38, NIV).

The idea of pastors leaving soul-winning work to gifted parishioners is a modern idea, not a New Testament command. We desperately need pastor-teachers, and God has given them to His Church. For lack of them, the world is filled with cults, confusion and heresy. But we need pastor-teachers who have a passion for the lost too.

Timothy, a godly pastor-teacher, was also admonished by Paul to "do the work of an evangelist" (II Timothy 4:5).

Riding the Pendulum

A friend of mine, a noted theologian and president of a seminary, gave a stirring message on this subject at a recent national meeting. The pastor, he said, was there to feed the flock, help them grow in Christ, keep them spiritually healthy, teach them to love one another, and train certain among them to reach nonbelievers. The shepherd, in other words, is to feed the sheep; it's up to the sheep to reproduce through soul winning.

The pastor, he added, should study a minimum of thirty-five hours a week, in order to be versed in the Scriptures well enough to carry out his duties effectively.

Isn't it interesting how we human beings seem to swing from one extreme to another? And it's no different in the evangelical church. At one time, not too many years ago, people expected the pastor to "do it all." After all, he was paid, trained and ordained, so he was expected to do the work of the ministry.

All of it.

Preaching. Teaching. Evangelizing. Visitation. Leading every committee and probably setting up the folding chairs and making the coffee for the fellowship meetings. That made about as much sense as a ball team sitting on the sidelines watching their coach play the whole game by himself!

Satan has managed for too long to convince Christian congregations that the pastor was to be the one who did all the outreach—and witnessing was not their responsibility.

Now the pendulum has swung the other way. Pastors have delegated much of the work of the ministry to the flock—and rightly so. But instead of using some of their time to reach nonbelievers in their community, they close themselves in their offices behind a word processor for thirty to forty hours of study a week.

That, I believe, is an error at the other extreme.

For many years, I was an evangelist, missionary, church planter, author and pastor, with no helpers at the beginning apart from my dear wife. Even for some time after God sent us workers, and men and women were added to the flock, I had to be the organizer, sustainer, administrator, pastor, Bible teacher, soul-winner, Sunday School teacher, lawn mower, wood chopper, and transportation provider—in addition to taking care of my family.

Studying thirty-five hours a week? Ridiculous. Impossible! I know many other pastors who would say the same thing. Only a large church with a designated staff could make such advice work.

As I thought and prayed about my seminary friend's teaching, God seemed to say to me, "Mac, think about the Great Shepherd, Jesus. He was the greatest teacher of all time. He taught His disciples impeccably—but not by sitting in His study. He led them in soul-winning. Any true pastor is not just a shepherd; he is also one of My sheep. Therefore, he is responsible to reproduce through soul-winning, as are all God's sheep. He should be out there bringing men and women to Christ, teaching and leading his flock to evangelize by example as well as word."

I believe God has called certain men and women with special gifts, with dedication and intelligence beyond the norm, to study the original languages of Scripture, to pore over every word, to defend the faith, and to help those of us who need assistance in understanding difficult passages. I know very well that the Holy Spirit is the true interpreter of the Word of God, but I also know that He has gifted some individuals to help us comprehend His precious truths.

I don't believe this is God's standard for all of us. In the long run, I don't think it seriously affects my spiritual life if I remember that Shallum was a Korahite. To this day, I am ashamed to say, I sometimes get the lineup of the kings of Israel and Judah confused.

I do believe these things are important . . . but not nearly as important as my personal relationship with Jesus. Or that His love for needy men and women should flow unhindered through me.

I came to this conclusion many years ago, when a friend of mine spoke at a church I had started. He was a professor at the seminary from which I graduated, and he said that no man should be a minister of the gospel unless he knew Greek and Hebrew. Later on, I challenged him, because of the unhappy feedback I'd been receiving from many parishioners at churches in the Pacific Northwest with pastors who were graduates of this excellent seminary.

There was no question that these young pastors were on fire for God, with a deep love for His Word. They were eager to share what they had learned, with earnest sincerity to serve, honor, and glorify the Lord. They were teaching their people—often with overhead projectors—"what the Greek said" about certain passages. And the people were getting discouraged. They told me, in effect, "There's no use in my reading the Bible for myself. I don't know Greek, so obviously I can't understand it." Time and again they were being "corrected" in their understanding of beloved Bible truths.

I wrote to my friend, the seminary president. "What are we doing?" I asked him. "Raising a bunch of Protestant popes? We can only understand the Word of God as the Greek students interpret it for us? Do we or do we not have accurate translations? Did God or did He not preserve His Word for us as He promised?"

I had similar observations to make to the professor from this seminary. I don't know Hebrew, and I know only a little Greek. Yet there is practically no doctrine in the Scriptures that I cannot understand either by searching the immediate context, or by comparing Scripture with Scripture. Millions of other Christians—including pastors—study the Word in the same way. Few pastors—even those who can spare time from their obligations to family and church to study some Greek or Hebrew—are really authorities on the original languages.

Some are called to this linguistic work, thank God, and I happily feed off them. Many of the real authorities are scholars who have spent years—even decades—in intense study of these languages. Their works are available to any pastor or interested Christian. So why should I become another one of the inexpert experts, in order to be a pastor?

I might add that if knowledge of the Word and the original languages makes better, more spiritual Christians, then how do we explain the deadness toward personal evangelism that is almost endemic in some of our seminaries—and unfortunately sometimes in the students they produce?

Part of the answer, I believe, lies in the motivation for study. Is it an academic exercise, an ego trip, a natural proclivity or curiosity, or a deep desire to know, love, and serve the Lord better?

I thank God for those indefatigable scholars whose dedication and study help preserve the unalloyed Word of God, and keep those of us who love Jesus informed and accurate in rightly dividing His Word. I enjoy using Greek language tools to supplement my understanding of difficult passages, or to enhance well-known texts. I can't wait to share new nuggets of truth from the Word of God as I discover them through this kind of study. The problem arises when this becomes an obsession—an end in itself—and when it keeps me from a passionate outreach for those outside of Christ.

Banquets and Beggars

I once spoke in a church of about seventy people in a large city in Pennsylvania. It seemed like a solid evangelical church, biblically well-grounded. The pastor assured me he was thrilled with the spiritual growth of his congregation. His people knew the Lord and were growing in the Word of God and in love for each other. Yet when I asked this pastor about their outreach to unbelievers, he said that few, if any, were coming to know the Lord Jesus Christ through their ministry.

Suddenly my heart felt like lead in my chest.

Thousands around them in that great city were on their way to Hell, while this little band of believers enjoyed their spiritual growth and fellowship. Imagine savoring a fantastic banquet, loaded with entrée after entrée, while starving beggars lying at the doors of the church can't get a crumb.

Sadly, this church represents thousands of others very much like it.

Of course every Christian ought to study the Word of God. It is our spiritual food. It is God's revelation, His love letter to us. Those who truly love Him must love His Word. Yet I can't help but note (as one who has read dozens of missionary stories and biographies) that often a people with just one, two, or three books of the Bible in their language live up to the limited light they have. With transformed lives and a deep hunger for the Word, these Christians demonstrate His love for unbelievers. They often seem to love and obey Jesus more than those of us who have the whole Word of God.

I remember so well meeting a man from a primitive tribe whose life had been transformed by the Word of Christ. He and his tribe had given up the worship of alligators, turtles and false gods. They had ceased to wage war and kill. They loved Jesus. Several had been martyred as they sought to reach neighboring peoples for Christ. Yet at that time only one book—Mark's Gospel—had been translated into their language.

Then I think of the early Christians, who had only the Old Testament and perhaps a few newly written books of the New Testament. Yet through those years some of the most devoted, powerful, Christ-glorifying men and women of all time spread the gospel with a compassion and boldness unmatched today.

I do not by any means believe the common cry today, "Christ is all that counts; doctrine only divides; love everybody, and never condemn anything or anybody." That is patently false. We are not to live by bread alone, but by every word of the Word of God. Bible study, through God's grace, will enhance our outreach. As we draw closer to Him, as we pray and grow in obedience to His will, we will be increasingly empowered by the Holy Spirit to become bolder and more effective in our witnessing.

Occasionally we see soul-winners who are not deeply spiritual in other areas of their lives. Sooner or later, their lack of a firm foundation and intimacy with the Savior through the Word will destroy them or their witness—or at the very least dull their effectiveness. Study and prayer are vital underpinnings to a life of sharing the love of Jesus Christ.

But even as we seek to explore and study and savor the wondrous Word of God, none of us need to be intimidated in our witness for Christ if we can't cross every "t" and dot every "i" from Genesis to Revelation. We must never allow any kind of study—even of the Bible—to become a substitute for impassioned soul-winning.

What will we trade for the souls of others, now that we are saved? The devil knows our price. Millions of professing Christians are trading with Satan for something they value more than the souls of men. It might be possessions, prestige, or power. It might be the balm of religious activity, soothing our conscience while our friends and neighbors die—lost. Whatever the diversion is, it's working.

What will you trade for a soul? Suppose Christians were offered one hundred thousand dollars for every soul they won to Christ. You and I know what would happen. Pastors and soul-winners would be besieged for soul-winning training. Thousands, perhaps millions, would be urgently seeking souls and pursuing the lost. Other activities would be largely set aside. If this is true, God forgive us for our lack of real love for Jesus and for souls. Again, what do you value most on this earth? What will you trade for a soul?

Moving Heaven and Hell

Chapter Six

For the love of Christ compels us.

II Corinthians 5:14

Years ago, I came across this tragic true story.

Every morning, a man and his wife rowed out to the middle of a large lake so that he could swim in the deep water. He couldn't swim far, so it was vital that his wife stay close to him with the rowboat. One morning, after he climbed into the water for his swim, she deliberately began to row away from him. He begged her to come back, but she kept on rowing away. Gasping and fighting for air, the man slowly slipped beneath the waves, pleading desperately until the water drowned out his voice. The wife returned to shore and drove their car back home, confident that in this isolated place she had committed the perfect crime.

The couple had a son, however, who had taken a job at a lookout tower some distance away. He happened to be using his field glasses at that moment, and saw his mother and dad row out on the lake. With increasing horror, he watched the whole scenario.

The son went to a lawyer, gave him the details, and asked, "Can my mother be prosecuted for the murder of my father?"

The lawyer consulted his weighty tomes, searching for a precedent in this unusual case. At last he said, "Yes, indeed she can. When someone has the means at their disposal to deliver another person who otherwise would die, and fails to use it, they can be prosecuted for murder."

What then, shall we say about those of us who have known Jesus Christ as Savior for years and years, but refuse to bear witness for His name? We know that one of the principle reasons God leaves His children on this world is to hold high our lamps, so that those in darkness might be brought into the light. The apostle James tells us, "Therefore, to him who knows to do good and does not do it, to him it is sin" (James 4:17).

If Jesus, heaven and Hell cannot move a person by the Holy Spirit to reach out to lost men and women, or even to obey His simple command, where is there any real love for Him, or for one's neighbor?

Believe me, I understand it isn't easy!

One Cold Alaska Night

I remember one particular night when my wife and I were missionaries in Alaska. As native Southerners, both of us suffered from the cold. On this particular night, the temperature had already dipped to twenty below zero. Snug and warm in my little home, I wanted nothing more than to relax and curl up with a good book. Or maybe watch a little TV.

But I couldn't relax. I felt a nagging unease in my conscience. I seemed to hear the Lord saying to me, *Mac, what are you doing tonight?*

"Lord, I've been out to church already three nights this week, and one other night I went calling."

But there was that voice again. *Mac, I asked what you're doing tonight.*

I hesitated. The Lord didn't.

Mac, you've already had two nights of R and R this week. Aren't you the one who goes all over the country talking about witnessing?

I was getting a little nervous—until I thought of a good, classic, biblical answer. "Lord, the Bible plainly says that we're to provide for our own. That means not only groceries, but love and companionship, right? I want to spend the night at home with my wife."

Mac, if you carried out your original plan, you'd have your nose in a book all evening. Virginia would barely get to see you.

I mounted one final, desperate plea. "Lord, it's twenty below outside. My car will never start."

Try it.

I shrugged on my warmest coat, picked up my Bible, and stumbled reluctantly to my car. I knew it wouldn't start, but I had to deal with that insistent voice inside. Shivering, I climbed behind the wheel and turned the key. Sure enough, the engine made an icy, grinding noise, but wouldn't start. Yes! I knew it! Now I could return to my chair and my book with a clear conscience. Then I turned the key one last time. Barooom…barooom. Defying all odds, the engine leaped to life, robbing me of my last excuse.

I decided to begin what I used to call "raw-knuckling"—knocking on strange doors in places where I'd never been. The term was especially apt on a cold night in Alaska. I stopped at a darkened house, with only one little light glowing inside. Knocking on the door, I wondered if it was a sin to hope that no one would answer. Before turning to leave, I knocked one last time. Suddenly I heard footsteps that sounded like the coming of King Kong in the cold darkness. The door jerked open, and I found myself face-to-face with a burly man who literally filled the doorway. He seemed at least ten feet tall.

"What d'you want?" he thundered.

What I wanted at that moment was to go home! Instead, I said, "Sir, I'm from the local church. I'm out calling tonight for the Lord Jesus Christ. May I come in for a few minutes and share with you about Him?"

Surprisingly, the big man stepped aside and motioned me in. After a few minutes of getting acquainted, I gently escalated the conversation to talking about his relationship to Jesus Christ. I looked him squarely in the eyes and said, "God loves you, and so do I. May I share with you from the Bible how to find salvation—and know for sure that you'll go to heaven when you die?"

The Holy Spirit began to do His work as I read those salvation verses to him. He opened his heart gladly, and prayed to receive Jesus Christ as his Lord and Savior. Suddenly I didn't feel the cold anymore. I didn't care about my book by my easy chair, or what television programs I may have missed.

I was bursting with a joy I simply could not contain.

Even if the man hadn't come to Jesus, I would have found myself loving him and praying earnestly for him. But he did receive the Lord, and that night he became my eternal brother in Christ.

Love by Faith

One vital item I left out of that story: Before I stepped out into the cold, I told the Lord exactly what was in my heart. I told Him I really didn't want to go, and asked for His forgiveness. I asked Him to fill me with His Holy Spirit, and claimed that filling by faith. I asked Him to love whomever I witnessed to through me, and involve me in that love. I told Him I would tell the person that I loved him or her, by faith, and unless He made it real, I would be a hypocrite.

I had only been witnessing to that rough-looking man for a few minutes when I began genuinely to love him. I found myself deeply wanting him to understand God's love and His offer of eternal life in Jesus. It had begun as "loving by faith," but quickly became loving in fact.

This determination to "love by faith" works in marriage, church, and in many other ways besides personal evangelism. By God's love and grace it has kept me winning souls for nearly forty-eight years. The truth is, I simply don't depend on how I feel on any given day or night. Yes, there are those times when I just can't wait to get out and share the Good News. Sometimes my heart feels so heavy for lost men and women that I can't contain myself. At other times I'm too comfortable, too busy, and have little or no desire in my heart to talk to people. So I ask for forgiveness. I ask for the filling of His Holy Spirit, and for Him to love through me. Then I go out to love by faith those who need Jesus, acting toward them as if I loved them, telling them that I love them . . . and He makes it real.

As those who are risen with Christ, who are dead to self, we need to heed this admonition: "Set your mind on things above, not on things on the earth" (Colossians 3:2). This is the backbone to a life of outreach. We are told pointedly not to love the world and its twisted philosophies, its lusts of the flesh, its eyes filled with desires, its boastful pride of life—and that those who do so do not have the love of the Father in them (I John 2:15–17).

Go out into the harvest fields. You can't raise a corn crop in your living room, or catch fish in your bathtub. Look at the broken people. They need Jesus here and in the hereafter. Let Jesus break your heart over them as His own heart is broken.

One of the greatest motivations to personal evangelism comes as you begin to see God work in the lives of those with whom you have shared Christ.

Years ago, I held evangelistic meetings in a rural area of New England, witnessing door-to-door during the days and preaching in the evenings. There was no regular pastor, so one of the farmers volunteered to go with me to the scattered farmhouses in the community. Over three days we led several people to Christ. We had really been beating the bushes, and by the last day I was exhausted. I needed an hour or two to work on my message, time to pray, rest, and grab a bite to eat. I was so hungry I felt weak.

As we headed for the house where I was staying, the farmer said, "Brother Mac, would you go with me to see a friend? He's seventy years old and a leading Jehovah's Witness."

I groaned (inwardly, I hope). Did the farmer just want to see an argument? He said his friend was a longtime JW and adamant in his beliefs. I knew it was impossible, in any ordinary situation, to lead a committed cultist to Christ in one visit. "Do you really love him?" I asked. "Have you been praying for him?"

"Yes, I have!" he answered. So on we went to this man's house, while I prayed for physical and spiritual strength. Although I spoke gently and carefully to the man, he got riled up as I countered some of his beliefs with simple statements from the Bible. He almost pranced back and forth, vehemently stating his stand against the Trinity, speaking of the theocratic kingdom on earth and other Jehovah's Witness doctrines.

At last I said, "Jim, God really does love you, and Jesus Christ really did die on that horrible cross to save you. Won't you please let Him?" The man's pacing slowed down, and I repeated the statement several times.

Abruptly, he stopped and looked at me. I had to go; my time was more than up. I said softly, "Jim, won't you please come and hear me preach tonight?"

He said slowly, "Yes, I believe I will." Jim came that evening, and soon afterward came to Christ. He gave his testimony as a new Christian to a four-state denominational convention just a few weeks later.

Only God could do that.

"Salvation is of the LORD" (Jonah 2:9).

Not only did the little church come alive in that area and the joy of Jesus flood the convention, but a certain farmer will believe in and practice personal witnessing for the true Lord and Savior, Jesus Christ, for the rest of his life.

Transformed Lives

In Anchorage, Alaska, I led the handsome thirty-two-year-old chef at the Captain Cook Hotel to Christ. (Later he married a former Miss Hawaii and became an evangelist.)

He brought a beautiful young singer-entertainer named Danielle out to a meeting. As I talked to her, she wept her way back to the Christ she had received as a young girl.

At the time, Danielle was living with the other half of her duo, an attractive, charming singer named Bill Robertson. After her recommitment to Christ, she and I went to work on Bill.

Bill was tremendously popular and on the way up in his career. "I'm not interested," he told me in no uncertain tones when I contacted him. I asked if he would at least listen to a tape of a sermon I had just preached on the fear of God, and he agreed.

About a week later, I called him back. "Are you interested enough for me to talk to you now?" He said yes, and received Jesus as his Savior at our first meeting. I insisted that he and Danielle remain apart until I married them, a week or so later. They agreed, and I performed the marriage. For a while they continued singing in the nightclub of the Captain Cook Hotel, cleaning up their act and coming down between sets to witness to the startled patrons.

One night they called me with an urgent request to help witness to Mark, a college senior who was on hard drugs and suicidal. I showed this young man how God loved him, and told him that Christ could not only save his soul but deliver him instantly from his drug habit. Mark received Christ, was delivered from his addiction and soon led his lovely Filipino girlfriend to the Lord. He went on to seminary and became a minister—a transformed junkie leading people to know Jesus Christ and grow in Him.

Bill and Danielle took my new convert and witnessing classes, and soon they were leading people to Christ themselves. They were hungry to grow in the Word, so they took a special cram course for a year at Western Baptist Seminary. After venturing into several ministry areas, Bill eventually began a highly successful swimming pool service in California. For a while, he also taught in John McArthur's Grace Community Church. He and Danielle continue to lead many people to Christ. They have two fine young sons who also love the Lord.

Recently, Bill called to tell me about a man they led to Christ, Steve Russo. Steve is on fire for the Lord, winning thousands of youth in the public schools. He is only one of many who have become powerful personal evangelists after Bill and Danielle led them to Jesus. As Bill once said, "Mac, you sure have a lot of spiritual grandchildren."

Another man I met in Alaska, Bruce Anderson, was a religious leader in a church—a big guy, powerful, angry . . . and lost. His wife, son and daughter had just come to Christ in some meetings I was holding. Bruce felt that his wife had made a fool of herself because she witnessed to about fifty people on her milk route the day after her conversion.

I said to him, "Let me show you what your wife is so excited about." It was amazing to see how God calmed him down as I read the salvation Scriptures and shared the gospel with him. He wanted to receive Christ but refused to bow his head or close his eyes to pray. I stuck out my hand and said, "Bruce, God promised to save you if you will call on Jesus Christ from your heart." I asked him if he would say, "Lord Jesus Christ, I now receive You as my personal Lord and Savior." He did. Then I asked him to repeat out loud three times with me, "He who believes in the Son has everlasting life" (John 3:36).

And he did.

Bruce and his family led dozens of people to Christ. After some study and training, Bruce planted two churches and helped start another, eventually pastoring a congregation on the Kenai Peninsula. Bruce Jr., fourteen years old when he was saved, made a great impact witnessing in his school in Homer. Later he went to Chile as a missionary, and eventually he became one of the deans in the Los Angeles Baptist Seminary.

Anyone can become a soul-winner. I knew a strong, volatile man in Anchorage named Darriel Barber. He told me how he had once tried to commit suicide by ramming his car—with all his family in it—into a bridge abutment. When I met Darriel, he believed he was a Christian but wasn't certain. So I led him by the Word of God to an assurance of his salvation. I then told him that any Christian both could and should win others to Jesus Christ.

For over two years I trained Darriel, and often took him out visiting with me. But he was never able to win one person to Christ. One night he broke down and sobbed. "You must be wrong, Mac. I can't do this. I've tried so hard." He had tried hard, and I had tried to direct him without discouraging him. But I won't even begin to illustrate how many ways he caused offense, stuck his foot in his mouth, and bungled his presentations.

I pleaded with him not to give up, reminding him that Psalm 126:6 was and is true. And just a short time later, Darriel was exhilarated, bouncing with joy, after leading two families to Christ. He became so filled with the desire to present Christ to lost men and women that he laid aside all his plans and went into the ministry. He and his staff in a church in Simi Valley, California, working in concert with Child Evangelism Fellowship, led seven hundred people to Christ in one year.

After Darriel died of a heart attack, his widow told me, "Mac, he never lost the vision. He was winning souls right up to the end of his life."

Anybody can lead others to Christ.

After a meeting I held in New York State, a Lutheran man became very concerned about reaching those outside of Christ. As a result, he launched a large music ministry and built a new concert hall in Albany. Their purpose was to reach people for Christ through music and testimonies given at the concerts. He told me excitedly over coffee some time ago that for many years they averaged leading nine hundred people a year to Jesus Christ.

In Detroit, Michigan, a lady made a similar decision to get serious about personal evangelism after I spoke at her church. When I returned a few years later, the church was still agog with what the Lord had done through that one woman. She had led two hundred people to Jesus. That's the power of the Word of God through a willing servant of God.

Dr. Mark Williams, who now pastors a church in a resort area of California, is one of the most evangelistic-minded pastors I know. A former associate of Christian apologist Josh McDowell, he began as a new pastor by accompanying me door-to-door to learn about witnessing. After several successful years in his first pastorate, Mark moved on to found another church. In one year, he had eighty new converts! He was soon called to a world-wide ministry as an advisor and trainer in church planting. Mark's wife, Carolyn, is a naturally shy lady. But seeing the Lord use her husband in evangelism gave her the hunger to get in on the action. On my last visit with her, she excitedly told me about three individuals she had been privileged to lead to Christ.

Together, Virginia and I nurtured and encouraged another young pastor and his wife from Pendleton, Oregon. Mike already had a strong desire to tell others about Jesus, but he was frustrated. His church was small, and the community seemed unresponsive to this young fireball. After spending time with that dear couple, Mike's desire to reach lost men and women really exploded. With our encouragement and God's apparent leading, Mike went to Brazil as a missionary.

When health problems closed the door to that opportunity after a couple of years, Mike became a visitation pastor in a church in Redding, California. Then, through the efforts of a good friend of his, Dr. Tim Blanchard, Mike became the director of evangelism for the Conservative Baptist Association of America. After a time there, Mike Silva branched off on his own in evangelism, and in a recent one-day meeting led seventeen hundred men to Jesus Christ! Mike also spoke at a meeting of the Fellowship of Christian Athletes, and God worked there too.

Franklin Graham just gave Mike his wholehearted endorsement. Franklin Graham, Billy's son, is a good friend of my son, Rocky McElveen, founder/owner of Alaskan Adventures. Franklin is a worldwide warrior for Jesus Christ, risking his life to start and support churches in Muslim nations. (Get his great book, "The Name!") We never know where it will end when we consistently lead people to Christ, and when we challenge, encourage, and train others to be soul-winners, whether one-on-one in personal evangelism or in a wider outreach. Seeing the change when Jesus saves even one person should give us an insatiable thirst to win others. Jesus loves souls. That is what He died for. Real Christians want to please Him by winning souls to Him for His eternal glory and their good.

We never know where it will end when we consistently lead people to Christ, and when we challenge, encourage, and train others to be soul-winners. Seeing the change when Jesus saves even one person should give us an insatiable thirst to win others. Jesus loves men and women, boys and girls. He gave His life to open a door of eternal salvation to all who believe. Those who belong to Him want to please Him by winning souls to Him for His eternal glory and their good.

Never Give Up!

Chapter Seven

You need to persevere so that when you have done the will of God, you will receive what he has promised. For in just a very little while, "He who is coming will come and will not delay."

Hebrews 10:36–37, NIV

One of the greatest discouragements for anyone involved in personal evangelism is seeing people make a profession of faith in Christ but neglect or refuse to associate with a Christian fellowship or follow through with baptism. They go on leading the same old life, and yet say they meant it when they asked Christ to save them.

Move over, friend—it breaks my heart too.

Realistically, there will always be defectors, false converts. Jesus said that would be true and it is. One of the twelve He trained was not truly one of them and betrayed Him. In the parable of the seed and the sower in Luke 8, only one out of four continued to follow the Lord. Luke 8:13 even tells of some who "have no root, who believe for a while and in time of temptation fall away."

There is a type of "faith," then, that is not saving faith. It is a belief that falls short of real salvation and will eventually be exposed. So many followers deserted the Lord at one point that Jesus said to his inner ring of disciples, "Do you also want to go away?" (John 6:67). Scripture says that Simon the magician "believed" in Jesus. Yet the apostle Paul rebuked him with the words, "You have neither part nor portion in this matter, for your heart is not right in the sight of God" (Acts 8:21). Had he been truly born again? It certainly doesn't sound like it!

At one point in Paul's mighty ministry, the apostle said, "At my first defense no one stood with me, but all forsook me" (II Timothy 4:16). We are warned that the love of many will grow cold, and that Satan will plant weeds among the wheat.

My best advice is to do the most thorough job you can in prayerfully presenting the gospel, including repentance and faith in Jesus as Lord and Savior. Ask these individuals if they really want Jesus to come into their lives and change them from the inside out. Make it clear that they cannot have the pardon without the Person—without Jesus. When they do make a decision, do the best you can to disciple them or get them discipled. Show them that real Christians, however inadequate, have a new pattern of life and a growing desire to obey the Lord (II Corinthians 5:17).

Australian evangelist Roy Comfort has said that it is easy to get apparent results with our man-centered gospel—one that lures people to "put on" Jesus, with the assurance that He will greatly improve this life with love, joy, peace—and perhaps other goodies like health and wealth. Instead, they find persecution, trials and humiliation, and become bitter backsliders. Peace and joy are legitimate fruits of salvation, but not to be presented in place of the need for repentance and salvation.

The person who receives the true gospel is satisfied. He faces no future punishment, and looks forward to an eternity in heaven. He is filled with gratitude and love.

The true doctrine is: "Once changed by Christ, always changed by Christ." The Bible says that those who have been born again have passed from death to life, from darkness to light, from being a child of Satan to being a child of God. He has "rescued us from the domain of darkness, and transferred us to the kingdom of His beloved Son" (Colossians 1:13, NASB).

We have been redeemed by His shed blood and made new creations in Christ. "Old things have passed away; behold, all things have become new" (II Corinthians 5:17).

We are saved by grace, and God describes clearly what true biblical grace is: "For the grace of God has appeared, bringing salvation to all men, instructing us to deny ungodliness and worldly desires and to live sensibly, righteously and godly in the present age, looking for the blessed hope and the appearing of the glory of our great God and Savior, Christ Jesus, who gave Himself for us to redeem us from every lawless deed, and to purify for Himself a people for His own possession, zealous for good deeds" (Titus 2:11–14, NASB).

This alone is true grace and true salvation. God says so.

Never give up because some do not follow through. I certainly have met my share of those who professed faith in my presence, but went on to break my heart. But I can also point to hundreds whose lives have changed because I did not give up!

Not everybody upon receiving the Lord reacts in the same way—or at the same speed. I led a soldier named Dusty to Jesus after debating Christianity with a whole roomful of soldiers. A few months later, I saw Dusty, drunk, in downtown Anchorage where I was doing some street preaching. I was sick at heart, and certain that his confession of Christ hadn't been sincere. But sometime later I got a letter from Dusty saying, "Mac, I tried to turn back to the old life, but I just couldn't do it. I really meant it when I accepted Jesus Christ." Some years later Dusty became an evangelist, and came with his touring group to speak at a church I had started in Burley, Idaho.

Another "tough guy" I led to Christ, a husky, handsome young man named Larry, dropped out of church after only a few weeks. I probably visited him ten or twenty times, but with no assurance that he was really hearing me. I prayed for Larry for over two years. Finally, late one Saturday night after preparing the message for Sunday morning, I began to scratch out names on my prayer list. I do this after a while, if there is no answer and I cease to be burdened—otherwise the list would grow impossibly bulky. I came to Larry's name and started to cross it out. He obviously wasn't interested, and I'd heard he was drinking.

But I couldn't pull my pencil through the name.

I hadn't had that trouble with any of the other names. Chagrined, I said, "All right, Lord, but if he's not in church tomorrow morning, I will scratch his name out."

As I got into the pulpit Sunday morning, there, up front and up close, was Larry! From that day on, he took off like a house on fire for the Lord.

Later on, I asked him what happened, and he said, "Mac, when I was saved you told me to walk by faith and not by feeling. But I grew up in a Pentecostal church, and there was a great deal of emotion. I kept waiting for that 'feeling' and it never came. So finally I said, 'Well, I'm going to try it Mac's way. I'm simply going to believe that Jesus did come into my heart at my request, as the Word of God says He did, even though I don't feel anything. I'm going to follow Jesus by faith and not by feeling!'"

Larry went on to Bible college in Minnesota, and eventually he became a stalwart preacher of the gospel. Incidentally, the great joy Larry couldn't seem to find as a new convert has filled his heart again and again as he walks with Jesus by faith.

So don't give up. Don't ever give up! No matter who drops out and who keeps going. Some will be false converts, as I John 2:19 makes clear. But others will follow Jesus through all the hills and canyons, all the valleys and vistas of the Christian life. And they will tell you until their dying day that life changed forever when you took the risk to introduce them to Jesus.

Look to the Fields

Chapter Eight

Be merciful to those who doubt; snatch others from the fire and save them; to others show mercy, mixed with fear—hating even the clothing stained by corrupted flesh.

Jude 1:22–23, NIV

Look to the Fields

Every Christian needs a scheduled time in his or her life to go out sharing the Good News. Pick a night and enlist a friend to go with you. Let nothing else interfere. Don't consider missing your witness time any more than you would consider missing worship on Sunday morning.

A farmer has a set time and place to plant his seed. What if he just put the seed in his pocket with a tiny hole in it, and asked God to sow it wherever He wanted a crop? We are to sow the seed anywhere and everywhere, but much more systematically—on ground that has been prepared and tilled by prayer.

Your home is one of the best evangelistic fields in the world. Inviting neighbors in for coffee and cookies, brunch, lunch, or dinner provides an excellent climate for sharing Christ in an informal, non-intimidating way.

During our time in Alaska, Virginia and I made a ministry out of inviting people over to eat. From roast moose to freshly baked bread to wild blueberry crunch, Virginia and I prepared the meals and opened our home, and only the Lord knows how many people came to Christ after those warm and friendly visits under our roof.

On Saturday mornings we invited servicemen and people from college and high school—sometimes twenty or more—over for a breakfast of pancakes and homemade berry syrup. For hours we talked and laughed together, playing games inside or out, depending on the weather. Then one of the new converts in the group would give a three-minute testimony about Jesus and his or her salvation, after which I would tell the group, "Virginia and I will be around. Just tell us if you want to talk to us about Christ, about how you can be saved and know it." Many came to Christ in this way, and then wanted to share with others. Some experienced deliverance from addictions to drugs, alcohol and obsessions with sex. A number from those days went on to become pastors and Bible teachers.

At times Virginia and I opened our home to needy people. Once we had a couple of "incorrigible" boys with us for a year. Both of them came to Christ. Many others, both adults and youth, came for weeks and months at a time.

Witnessing Without Limit

There are countless ways to present the Good News. You can put your personal testimony on tape or video and give it out to friends, family or any people you have contact with during the week. But you must follow it up with a personal visit. You can give out books or tracts; you can give parties for your neighbors and show Christian videos that tell how to be saved—but again, personal follow-up is essential.

Evangelistic Bible studies are an excellent means for leading people to Jesus. My son Randy excels at this, and he has started churches with the converts from such studies. He has developed his own matriculation process so that usually, after a certain number of Bible studies, a well-informed inquirer receives Jesus and continues on in the study until he is well versed in Bible basics and in Christ.

If you know a good, reliable Bible teacher or evangelist on television, invite someone who needs Christ to watch the program with you, and then follow through when it's over. You can now reach people with a website, or over the Internet!

Then there is phone evangelism. I have used the phone to lead people to Christ many times—friends, acquaintances, and complete strangers. In Kenai, Alaska, I led a distraught man named George to Jesus Christ. His wife had just taken their child and left for the Lower Forty-Eight, vowing never to come back. I asked him to call her, telling him I would help pay for the call. I spoke briefly to George's wife, telling her what had just happened. Then George brokenly shared his testimony with her. Afterward, I took the phone back and tenderly, compassionately told this dear lady how she could come to know Christ and have her shattered heart and splintered family healed. I told her how she could be saved by trusting Jesus alone for her salvation. How sweet it was to hear her pray to receive Christ over the phone.

Subsequently, she flew back to her husband. They became witnesses for Christ. At a new converts' banquet we held a year or two later, George told about how he had since led thirteen people to Jesus Christ, including his own father, who had also become passionate about introducing others to Christ.

Witness everywhere and anytime the opportunity presents itself; on the job, in recreation, in the neighborhood, on planes, trains, buses, boats, grocery stores, wherever. Newspaper ads can be used to make contacts. I know. I've done it. You can too.

A lady I led to the Lord in Cooper Landing, Alaska, began a letter-writing ministry to non-Christian inmates in jail. She also learned to read Braille, and translated the Bible and salvation booklets into Braille for blind people.

Children's clubs, whether run over a weekend, a week, or weekly over several months, can draw many to Christ, particularly from unchurched backgrounds. Offer crafts, baking, sports, teen activities—and of course Bible study—for kids of all ages. You can do it.

Win your neighbors with friendship evangelism—as long as you keep the ultimate purpose well in mind. Invite them out for lunch, and introduce them to Jesus in a nonthreatening, neutral atmosphere. Use your hobbies for Christ. Sharing activities breaks the ice and opens the door for witnessing—bowling, golfing, checkers, sewing, ceramics, you name it. I've led people to Christ through hunting or fishing with them.

Visit newcomers in town. Take them homemade rolls or a casserole. Make friends. Invite them to your church. Visit church contacts. Visit people in the hospital. Visit nursing homes—everyone you meet needs love, and some of them need Christ.

Go door-to-door with a simple, honest loving request to share something wonderful that has changed your life—Jesus Christ.

Go with a group, or a partner, to give out tracts or booklets at a public event, or on a crowded street corner.

Gather several brave souls together and go street witnessing, or get a microphone and give your testimony and tell how Jesus shed His blood on the cross, dying in our place, rising bodily from the grave, and now offers His free and forever salvation to those who receive Him.

At the very least, always carry tracts with you. If you are extremely shy, slip them surreptitiously into rest rooms, post offices and places where people gather. Leave them with your (generous please) tip at restaurants. Sooner or later, someone is going to catch you, and you are going to have to begin witnessing. "Let the redeemed of the Lord say so" (Psalm 107:2)!

Keep looking for new fields to harvest, new contacts to make. Jesus said to His disciples that if one town rejected their witness they were to go on to another. The possibilities and opportunities are endless. Ask God to open them up for you, and you'll think of other methods as well as these. Commit yourself to reaching people for Christ.

If you don't like my ways in sharing Christ, do it your way. If you don't care for my approach, develop your own approach.

If you don't approve of my methods, choose your own methods. Just make sure you do it.

Truth and Love

Chapter Nine

"Go out into the highways and hedges, and compel them to come in, that my house may be filled."

Luke 14:23

Truth and Love

I had a friend named Errol when I was in seminary in Portland. Before he came to Christ, he was a tough taxi driver. One night in Portland, he picked up a young man who got in the seat behind him. Suddenly, Errol felt a gun barrel poking into his back! "Pull over!" the man demanded.

Errol did, shaking with terror. "Where will you go if I pull this trigger?" the gunman asked. "I—I d-don't know," Errol stammered.

"Turn around!" Errol did, and found out that the young man had simply stuck a finger in his back. He was a witnessing Christian.

Errol was furious. Considering his temper, it was a wonder he didn't kill the man, or at least beat him up. A few months later, however, while deer hunting, Errol found his thoughts in turmoil.

Conviction gripped his soul.

He put his gun down and sat on a log. There, alone in the quiet woods, Errol called on the Lord Jesus Christ and was born again. Now Errol knows where he would go if somebody pulled the trigger of a real gun on him. I don't exactly recommend this approach to witnessing. But isn't our Lord wonderful in the ways He uses us?

I once led an engineer to Jesus Christ. I had sized him up as easily offended, and deliberately avoided any kind of confrontation. He received Christ after a service one night, though I didn't know until he told me a few days later. He said he would never have responded to any kind of pressure—like coming forward at the service—and that nobody else could have led him to Christ.

I was curious. "Chuck," I asked, "did anyone else ever talk to you about Jesus?"

"Yes!" he said in disgust. "My very first day on the job when I was working my way through college, this guy walked up to me and said, 'Are you saved? If you're not saved you will die in your sins and go to Hell!'"

Chuck told me he even looked for another job. He resented mightily what he called this "crude, rude approach."

"Chuck," I said, "had you ever thought much about where you would go when you died—about Jesus or heaven and Hell?" He said no. "Did you think much about heaven and Hell and where you would spend eternity after this man offended you with his question?"

"All the time," he admitted.

"When we get to heaven," I said, "you may find that this man had as much, if not more, to do with your salvation than I did."

Of course I believe in using tact, speaking the truth in love, being gentle, and not offending. But Christians today are pushing that envelope further than the Bible ever did.

Never offend anyone, we're told,
with rudeness,
or aggressiveness,
or arrogance,

or condescension,
or a holier-than-thou attitude,
or by arguing about trivial things,
or raising your voice,
or in any other conscious way.

Nevertheless, offenses will come. They're bound to. And if we sought to avoid them all, we would never even open our mouths. The gospel of Christ will be offensive to some, no matter how gently you present it—because the Cross itself is an offense. It's impossible to make the message of the cross non-offensive without diluting, twisting or otherwise misrepresenting the truth. Jesus Himself was refuted, undercut, mocked, rejected, and eventually crucified—and it certainly wasn't because of any mistakes He made in witnessing.

Some will love you. Some will hate you. "For we are to God the fragrance of Christ among those who are being saved and among those who are perishing. To the one we are the aroma of death leading to death, and to the other the aroma of life leading to life. And who is sufficient for these things?" (II Corinthians 2:15–16).

Clearly, none of us are sufficient apart from the grace of God. And so, however you are received, love everyone you share with, and whatever the outcome, pray for them.

As a general principle, I believe it is best not to argue or dispute while seeking to present Christ. Nevertheless, I will, if that's the only way to get their attention. I once strongly debated with a young atheist scientist (who later became the head of Alaska's Fish and Game Department) for three hours. He came to Christ in the end, along with his wife, and they joined the church I had started in Anchorage.

Even when we may be called upon in witnessing to contend for the faith, we must always do so without being contentious, always speaking the truth in the love of Christ. There is a perverse manner of disputing which the Bible forbids for Christians (I Timothy 6:5), yet Paul reasoned, disputed, and taught the truth in Ephesus—first for three months in the synagogue, with heavy opposition, and then for two years daily, in the school of Tyrannus. People found salvation, a church was started, and "all who dwelt in Asia heard the word of the Lord Jesus, both Jews and Greeks" (Acts 19:10).

Many Methods

D. L. Moody, saved at seventeen, began to share Christ and win souls almost instantly, with some fairly unorthodox approaches to witnessing. A poorly educated man, he was a gentle but persistent giant. One day he attempted to witness on the sidewalk to the daughter of a barkeeper. She ran away, through the bar, with Moody in hot pursuit. She ran upstairs. Moody lumbered after her. She ran into her bedroom. So did Moody. She crawled under the bed. Moody dragged her out—and told her about Jesus. She received Christ and grew up to be a fine Christian lady, with several of her children going into full-time ministry.

Then there's Mordecai Ham, the man who led Billy Graham to Jesus Christ. One day Ham rode up to a farmer's house to witness to him. The man was out in his field plowing. He saw Ham coming from a good way off and, leaving his plow, ran and crawled into a haystack. Mordecai Ham rode up and saw a leg sticking out of the hay. Promptly dismounting, he walked across the field, dragged the farmer out, and led him to the Savior.

Granted, these may not be typical approaches to witnessing, but both of these men won souls. As Moody is said to have observed to an arrogant young man who criticized his methods, "I like the way I evangelize better than the way you don't evangelize."

One could easily make a biblical case for winning people to Christ upon the first contact. How many times in the New Testament do we read of Jesus or the disciples going back to a person to share Christ with them a second time? By the same token, however, we could just as easily make a case for slow biblical indoctrination and then conversion, as probably occurred in the school of Tyrannus.

We could say a person has to pray a certain prayer in a certain way to receive salvation. In the Old Testament God demanded, "Look to Me, and be saved, all you ends of the earth!" (Isaiah 45:22). In the Gospels we have the record of a brief and poignant prayer: "God, be merciful to me a sinner" (Luke 18:13). God heard the man's prayer, and he was saved.

We may have a legitimate concern about "picking green fruit"—pushing and urging men and women to pray to receive Christ before their hearts have been prepared by the Holy Spirit. That's all well and good—we want true spiritual conversions, not shallow emotional responses that will wither away in the first light of a new day. But we should have an equal concern about persuading—even compelling—people to come to Jesus Christ, for that is scriptural also. "Behold, now is the accepted time; behold, now is the day of salvation" (II Corinthians 6:2, KJV).

There is no "salvation formula" prayer. And though I try to guide people carefully in the things they must believe, and even have some words I look for in their salvation prayer, some are saved who do not use those words, and some are not saved who do use those words. Salvation depends upon their heart, not their words—what they understand about themselves, and about the shed blood of Jesus Christ when they call on Him to save them. This only happens as the Holy Spirit acts through the Word of God on their heart. It is not intellect that wins souls.

One of God's saints—with the most consistent joy in outreach that I have ever seen—is a fellow in my home church who is considered "borderline mentally challenged." Yet his attitude and love for Jesus is absolutely contagious. He has shown all of us in the church what God can do with someone who really loves Him, and loves to give witness for Him. Emmett fights physical problems, emotional depression, uncertain financial fluctuations, inability to hold a steady job, and other difficulties. But he consistently and continually shares Christ, and goes with anyone who will take him to witness for His Savior! He remembers and finds roads and addresses I can't find. In this, he is a genius!

Years ago I coached a quarterback, Q. C. Howard, and led him to Christ. Q. C.'s son Tim converted to Mormonism when he married a beautiful Mormon girl named Karen. Q. C. and his lovely wife, Bonita, prayed earnestly for their son and daughter-in-law. After some time, Tim and Karen came to see me, searching for spiritual truth, and both received the Lord Jesus Christ. They were baptized and we had some intense Bible studies together. Though they have been Christians for barely a year, they have already written a fine book on Mormonism to help others find their way out of the LDS deception.

Once you lead a man or woman to Christ and see his or her face begin to shine with His love, encourage your new convert to begin telling the story to others, while the fire of new joy is blazing hot.

I once fought like a Bengal tiger for the heart of a Christian Scientist woman in her early twenties. God's Holy Spirit moved, and Betty was saved. Her lovely face was even more radiant with the thrill of her conversion! The next morning I had a call from the airport in Anchorage, Alaska—Betty had flown in her younger sister so I could share Christ with her. This one was really tough, but she did make a profession of faith in Jesus Christ. Then Betty wanted to do the same with her brother—fly him in from California.

I began to teach Betty to witness, although in truth she needed very little instruction. She just needed to be unleashed! A few weeks later, I took her out with my wife and daughter to share Christ. We found ourselves in the neighborhood where a famous college professor lived. This was a man who had been on several expeditions to the South Pole—and had even had a mountain peak in Antarctica named for him and his brother. A number of local pastors and others had tried witnessing to this professor, but none had even dented his surface. He had taught in an extremely liberal college for years, and he scorned "fundamentalists" like us.

Remembering all this, I was most interested when I saw Betty come out of the professor's home, scrawling something on a note card.

"How did it go, Betty?" I asked.

"Oh," she said breezily, "he received Jesus."

"What?"

I was stunned. This lady was no more than a babe in Christ! As soon as I could, I went in to see the professor and his wife, who had also received the Savior. I said,

"Professor, how in the world did Betty manage to lead you to Jesus?"

He smiled at me. "That young lady was so enthused, so radiant with the love of Jesus Christ, that I knew it must be real."

Betty's husband Mike came home from his tour of duty in the military, and she led him to Jesus. They moved on back to the Lower Forty-Eight, and Betty called me up from time to time. She was always excited about the Lord, but once she sent me a tape on which she almost seemed to be sobbing.

She related that in her first year as a believer she had led only seventeen people to the Lord.

I wept too, but for a vastly different reason. If she only knew. Dear God, I prayed, please send us some more Bettys!

Today, Colonel Mike Hockett, Betty's husband and my treasured friend, live in Colorado. He and Betty came by not long ago to see Virginia and me in Mississippi. The fire still burns!

Revel in the love of Jesus, and let Him love lost souls to salvation through you. Other than being saved yourself, knowing and loving and being loved by Jesus, there is no greater joy in this world than that of showing another lost soul the only way home. Don't miss it.

A Final Appeal

Chapter Ten

And I appeal to you, brethren, bear with the word of exhortation, for I have written to you in few words.

Hebrews 13:22

A Final Appeal

Dear American Christian,

We are besieged by evolution, abortion, hedonism, crime, and a growing, increasingly aggressive Muslim world, which has conquered much of Asia and Europe, and is fast invading America.

We are riddled with cults, drugs, alcoholism, pornography and the rampant homosexual agenda. While Muslims, Mormons and Eastern religions expand in our once-Christian nation by leaps and bounds, many of God's children have been caught in the net of materialism and seeking "the good life." We pay little or no attention to the fact that God says covetousness is idolatry, and that no idolater "has any inheritance in the kingdom of Christ and God" (Ephesians 5:5).

Liberalism and intellectualism assail our Bible and seek to distort, dilute and destroy it. Sexual promiscuity ravages our families and our youth, and sexually transmitted diseases, not to mention AIDS, have become epidemic. Yet the most terrible malady affecting us is our apathy. While Christian churches close at the rate of thirty-five hundred to six thousand per year, mosques multiply exponentially. According to a recent survey, 88 percent of our youth in evangelical churches leave by age eighteen and never come back! Twenty-five thousand "evangelical" churches in a recent year did not report one baptism! Only 3 percent of professing Christians ever lead anyone to Christ. May God break our hearts, as His is broken too.

At the same time, youth in other countries are living and dying heroically for Jesus. Even as I write this, thousands of Christians worldwide are dying for Christ. Sudan, Indonesia, some parts of China, India, and Pakistan, much of Asia, and many Muslim countries persecute Christians to the death, often torturing them, raping the women, and making sex slaves of some of the women and children, unless they convert to Islam.

Little John Jedi, ten years old, living in Sudan, saw his mother, father, and four siblings brutally murdered before his eyes by Muslim soldiers. The Muslim soldiers captured John Jedi, and made him gather wood for a huge fire. They then tied his hands and his feet, and told him they would free him if he became a Muslim, but would burn him in the fire if he would not.

John Jedi said simply, "I am a Christian."

He was thrown into the fire and left for dead, but miraculously he escaped. I have seen pictures of his burned body and crippled arm. Today, still a young child but growing in his faith, he continues to declare, "I am a Christian."

All over the world youths and adults are putting their lives on the line for Jesus, with one hundred and fifty thousand expected to be martyred this year. Yet these persecuted believers can't keep their mouths shut about Jesus. They often pray for—and sometimes win—their Communist or Muslim tormentors to Christ. One week, Tim White of the organization Voice of the Martyrs told of some Afghans he met who had only been Christians for three months. "We are ready to die for Jesus!" they told him.

My dear, soft, beloved fellow American Christians, what is wrong with us that in a free country we make such little attempt to win men, women, and children to Jesus Christ? Please, let us lay aside all excuses, and plunge into this needy world with fervor and passion for Christ and for souls, while there is yet time.

God help us, save us, revive us and use us! There is no other hope but Jesus for this world or the next!

One editor shared this story about a woman, Greta, who was instrumental in her salvation. Greta was terminally ill—blind, in chronic pain, and hooked up to multiple drains, drips and catheters. She'd suffered a stroke and couldn't speak. She communicated by blinking her eyes for yes or no. Yet in the last weeks of her life, she won a young nurse to Christ and led a volunteer who had wandered from the faith into a new and vibrant relationship with the Lord.

Impossible? Not at all. Because Greta asked the volunteer—blink blink—to read to her every day from the Bible that was always on her bedside table. Reading from the living, active Word of God over those weeks fanned into flame again the faith she thought she had squashed years ago. Soon she was sharing Christ with other terminal patients.

Greta also communicated by humming. She might not have been able to speak, but almost anytime you went by her room you could hear her humming the hymns from her Christian Reformed upbringing. Whenever the nurse went in to care for Greta, she had to listen. At first it irritated her, as the familiar words from the rejected faith of her parents played over and over in her head. But after a while, she began asking Greta, "Do you still believe all those promises of Jesus?" Blink. (Yes.) "Even with what God has let happen to you?" Hard blink. (Yes!)

And so a young nurse was won to Christ by a sightless, speechless, dying Dutch woman—because she witnessed the reality of a faith that was being tested to the death.

So tell me, who among us cannot in some way reach out to the lost for Christ? Why do we give so much importance to the fleeting distractions in this sliver of time when all eternity yawns before us? Let's stop playing at church, playing religious games—for Jesus' sake, for our sake, and for the sake of lost men and women. No one ever said with his dying breath, "I'm sorry that I reached so many souls for Jesus."

God is a God of grace, and He will never withdraw His love from His true children. But He wants us to burn with His love; He wants our hearts to break over those outside of Jesus Christ.

The Son of Man came to seek and save the lost. And Jesus said, "As the Father has sent Me, I also send you" (John 20:21).

The "MAC" Approach

Chapter Eleven

Almost any approach you use for personal evangelism will consist of an introduction, presentation of the gospel, and the close, or invitation.

Let's say you're in conversation with a man you've never met before . . .

After a few minutes of talking—to relax the atmosphere and build rapport—gently accelerate the conversation into the spiritual realm by asking about his church background. Is he presently attending a church, and if so, where? Most people don't take offense or feel threatened at these questions, and you can learn a great deal about them from their response. More important, you are creating a climate favorable to the working of the Holy Spirit as He plants the seed—the Word of God—in that person's heart.

At the right moment, say politely, "Do you mind if I ask you a personal question?" When you ask permission first, he cannot in all honesty say you are "forcing religion" on him. Almost invariably the answer is yes. If he demurs, have a friendly visit and leave, praying for a more propitious time.

Once you've been given permission to ask, use a version of the following: "Mr. Smith, suppose you were to die to-night. What would you say when God asked you why He should let you into heaven?"

Listen carefully to the response. (You may have to recite the answer back to him later on.) See if he is trusting in Jesus—in Jesus alone—for his salvation, or in good works alone, or in Jesus plus good works. If there is any doubt whatsoever, present Christ. Tell him you have some good news to share with him, so that he can know he has eternal salvation. You may wish to quote or read him I John 5:13:

These things I have written to you who believe in the name of the Son of God, so that you may know that you have eternal life. NASB

Depending on the circumstances and the leading of the Holy Spirit, this may be a good time to give your testimony; tell him how you came to know for sure that you found salvation in Christ. Ask if you may share with him what the Bible says about how you can know that you are saved. If the situation permits, get him to read the verse from a Bible, booklet or tract out loud. In some special cases it may be best or necessary to quote the relevant verses from memory, explaining as you go along. Ask him to tell you what each verse says to him. Help him along, but carefully; listen to see if he understands the text, so you will know how to proceed.

These are the verses I have found most helpful, organized into what I call my "MAC" Approach: **M**an **A**ccept **C**hrist.

Man -- Man is a lost sinner (Romans 3:23; 6:23). Explain what sin is:

- Unbelief, which is going our own

way (Isaiah 53:6)

- Being self-centered instead of Christ-centered
- Being our own god

Mention the terrible danger of being eternally separated from God. We are sinners both by nature and by choice. Just as an apple tree bears apples because it is an apple tree, so we bear sins because by nature we are sinners. One apple tree may have a thousand apples on it; another may produce just one. But they are both still apple trees. So it is not how many sins we produce or whether we sin more or less than someone else. We are all lost sinners. Beating the apples off the tree will not change the nature of the tree. It is still an apple tree and will continue producing apples. Getting rid of some sins in our life does not change our basic nature.

If we are to become a child of God and get into heaven, our very nature must be changed. But we can't do it on our own. That is why we must be born again by the Holy Spirit.

Explain what grace is by showing clearly that:

- Religion cannot save
- Good works cannot save (Ephesians 2:8–9)
- Baptism cannot save

Ask, "Why did Jesus have to die if we could make ourselves good enough to go to heaven?"

Suppose a man drives right through a red traffic light. Suddenly, in his rearview mirror, he sees flashing blue lights. But when the officer pulls him over, the man says breezily, "Sir, I've driven through this intersection thousands of times on my way to work over the years. And every single time I've stopped when the light was red. So you can't tell me it really matters that this one time I disobeyed the law, can you?"

Would any policeman buy that line? Do you think God will?

Accept -- Show that we are not children of God. We have to be born again in order to become children of God (John 3:3; 1:12).

Explain who Jesus is, and what He did in shedding His blood on the cross, and rising again from the dead for us (I Corinthians 15:1–4; Colossians 1:13–14).

Explain that we must accept Him as Lord and Savior (Romans 10:9–10, 13).

- Define Lord (God, Leader, Boss, Manager, Owner).
- Demonstrate from Romans 10:13 how to call upon Him: "For whoever calls on the name of the LORD [*with belief*] shall be saved" (italics mine).
- Explain that faith is not just a head belief but a heart belief.

- It is not simply believing in a historical fact, like George Washington crossing the Delaware, or believing that Christ was crucified.
- Faith is commitment to a Person; it is a total surrendering of your body, heart, and mind to Jesus Christ as your Lord and Savior. The word belief has degenerated to mean nothing more than an opinion or an intellectual assent. But the Greek word for faith or belief in the New Testament implies much more. It carries the idea of "trusting in" or "relying upon." Far more than describing an opinion or simple agreement with a proposition, it involves commitment. True belief affects behavior. Saving faith in Christ produces a changed life. (See James 2:17–20.)
- Demonstrate from Romans 10:13 how to call with complete trust upon the Lord Jesus Christ to be saved: "For whoever calls on the name of the LORD shall be saved." Our part is to call with belief. His part is to save us.
- Ask, "Can God lie? Would He save you if you called on Jesus? Would Jesus, who loved you so much that He died, shedding His blood in agony on the cross for you, turn you down when you call on Him?" If you really call with belief on Jesus, God would have to save you, because He promised, and God cannot lie!

- Ask, "Do you understand clearly?"

Christ -- Ask, "Jesus loves you so much. Would you like to receive Him as your Lord and Savior right now?" If the answer is yes, ask, "Would you like to pray your own prayer, or do you want me to lead you?"

Here is a suggested pattern for a salvation prayer:

- Lord Jesus Christ, I am a lost sinner. Come into my heart and life and cleanse me from all sin by Your shed blood. I put my trust in You alone for my salvation. Make me a child of God, and let me know that I am saved, now and forever. I accept Your free gift of everlasting life. I receive You right now, Lord Jesus Christ, as my very own personal Lord and Savior. In Jesus' name, amen.
- Lead him at this point to a "know so" salvation (Romans 10:13; John 3:36; I John 5:13). Don't tell him that he now has salvation; show him these Scriptures until he knows for himself from the Word of God that he has been saved. Ask from Romans 10:13, "Did Jesus save you or did He lie? Which did He do, if you called out in belief, according to the Word of God?" Turn to John 3:36, and read it out loud with him three times. Then ask him to quote it. Ask him if he has now believed on

Jesus. Ask him what God's Word says he now has (everlasting life).

- Ask him if he could ever lose it. Ask him if he has everlasting life now (yes) or will only get it when he dies. Point to the present tense of the verb: has.
- Make sure that he understands that saving faith is trusting in Jesus Christ alone, by a definite decision at a point in time, for salvation. Ask him if he now knows, according to the Word of God, that he is saved. Ask him where he would go right now if he was to die. If he answers "heaven," then say, "Let's pray and thank Him out loud for salvation."
- Always have a person pray twice—once when receiving Jesus, and again to thank the Lord Jesus when he is sure of his salvation. This screens out many who have prayed but still aren't sure, and others who did it just as an experiment, or to please you, or simply to get you off their back.

This process gives the individual time to absorb the Word of God and come to biblical assurance by the Word and the Holy Spirit. When it is properly and prayerfully carried out, a higher percentage of those who make decisions are truly, scripturally converted—born again by the Spirit of God, not by human will or emotional pressure. There will in time be great joy and peace in those truly converted, but that does not always occur at the time of salvation. Again, faith is the root, and feeling the fruit, of salvation.

As soon as the person declares that he now knows, according to God's Word, that he has salvation, and has finished thanking God for saving him, take his hand and welcome him into the family of God.

Immediately share with your newborn believer the words of Jesus in John 14:23: "If anyone loves Me, he will keep My word; and My Father will love him, and We will come to him and make Our home with him." Emphasize that Jesus said if a person truly loves Him, he will keep His word. Not if, and, but, maybe, or if it is convenient. He will. God says so. Assure the new convert that you know he will want to show his love for Christ by obeying Him.

Make it absolutely clear that nothing he could have ever done—no matter how impressive his works for God or lifestyle changes—could have saved him or helped save him. Jesus paid it all! The proof of his salvation, however—the evidence—will be a new willingness, an eagerness, to obey in love and please the Lord Jesus Christ.

Before you leave, speak briefly about baptism, about his need to confess Christ before others, to read the Bible, pray, and gather with other believers for worship and teaching in the Word. Ask him to begin by reading the Gospel of John, and then I John. Some will benefit from a more contemporary translation of the Scriptures, such as the New American Standard Bible, the New King James and the New International Version.

Get a commitment from the new convert about baptism. If he was baptized before, perhaps as a child, show him why he needs to be baptized again. Show him that baptism comes after salvation, as an act of obedience (Acts 2:41; 10:47–48; 16:31–33). Assure him that the waters of baptism cannot wash away one sin; the blood of Jesus Christ has already done that if he is truly saved. God commanded baptism following salvation as an outward picture of an inward experience. Baptism also pictures our union with Christ in His death, burial and resurrection, and is symbolic of our being raised to new life in Christ.

Try to make another contact with a new convert within twenty-four to forty-eight hours. I have read surveys that say most converts seem to follow through if they are contacted early on in their new life. More than half "fade away" within a week, and up to 90 percent in about two weeks, if they are not contacted again.

Share I John 3:6–9 and explain that while a Christian can—and inevitably will—sin, a true Christian cannot live in sin (Hebrews 6:9). Teach him how to walk in the Spirit and not fulfill the lusts of the flesh (Galatians 5:16). Teach him how to have victory over sin (Romans 6:11; I Corinthians 15:57), to live by grace and not by the law. Show him his position in Christ (Hebrews 10:10–14) and his responsibility to conform his behavior to that position as he grows in the Lord. Teach and encourage him to confess instantly any sin in thought, word or deed, for unbroken fellowship with the Savior and with other Christians (Proverbs 28:13; I John 1:9).

Teach him to walk by faith and not by feeling, to let Jesus live His life through him (Galatians 2:20; Colossians 3:1–4).

Suggest that he enjoy Jesus and His salvation every single day. Ask him to thank the Lord Jesus Christ daily for dying on the cross and for saving him. Ask him to tell the Lord Jesus Christ that he loves Him—every single day.

Love should now begin to flood the new convert's life—love for Jesus, for other Christians, for the church, and for those outside of Jesus. There should be a hunger for the Word and for prayer, and an increasing desire for personal purity (II Corinthians 5:17).

As time goes on and you have opportunity, help him with his personal testimony, and encourage him to share Christ in his circle of friends and acquaintances. Encourage him to ask for and claim by faith the filling of the Holy Spirit, who always gives boldness and overcomes our fear in witnessing (Acts 4:8, 29–31).

Rejoice that another soul-winner for Christ has been born.

Here is my personal favorite plan because it is simple, easy to learn, effective, and inexpensive. I have used it to lead many hundreds over the years to the Lord Jesus Christ.

Man: Lost Sinner. Romans 3:23; 6:23; Isaiah 53:6. Grace. He cannot save himself. Ephesians 2:8–9.

Accept: New Birth. John 3:3; 1:12.

Christ: Who He Is, What He Did. Romans 10:9–10.

Lord and Savior.

Call on Jesus, Receive Him by Faith. Romans 10:13.

Turn from Self and Sin to Jesus.

Assurance: John 3:36; Romans 10:13; I John 5:13.

Supplemental verses as needed:

Jesus is God. Isaiah 9:6; John 1:1–3; 20:28.

Jesus shed His blood on the cross for us as our substitute. I Corinthians 15:1–4; Colossians 1:14; I Peter 2:24; I John 1:7.

Learn this outline so that you know it by heart. Learn these verses and also mark them in your Bible. Learn how to explain them clearly to those who are outside of Christ.

What follows is what I call a "soul-winner's checklist."

►Know that you are saved.

►Surrender your body to God and believe that God has accepted your body as a living sacrifice.

►Pray before going.

►Ask for and claim the filling of His Holy Spirit.

►Commit to Him all your fears and inadequacies.

►Learn to live by faith, not by feelings.

►Learn to love by faith.

►Be willing to be a fool for Christ in order to bring men and women to Him.

►Confess all known sin and forsake it..

►Claim God's wisdom, love, compassion and boldness.

►Carry your New Testament with you always.

►Check your breath; be clean and neat.

►Expect God to use you.

►Keep it simple. Have one person do the presentation.

- ►Present Jesus.
- ►Show key verses as well as quoting them.
- ►Be courteous. Never argue; listen well.
- ►Show them their hopelessness apart from Jesus Christ.
- ►Show clearly the need for repentance toward God.
- ►Demonstrate clearly from Scripture that Jesus is the only way.
- ►Anticipate objections; answer them before they come up.
- ►Stress the necessity of being certain of salvation.
- ►Stress the urgency of salvation.
- ►Highlight the joy of abundant life in Christ.
- ►Speak of the joy of abundant life in Christ.
- ►Cast a vision of the wonder and sweet solace of heaven.
- ►Warn of the eternal horror of Hell.
- ►Be very careful to stress the gift of salvation, the shed blood of the Lord Jesus Christ, and the need to trust in Him alone for salvation. Make sure they know who Jesus is: the eternal God, Creator, and Redeemer

Stories That Open Eyes

Many times in the Gospels, we see Jesus telling a simple story to illustrate some profound, eternal truth. Storytelling may also help us in our presentation of the gospel. Using such a story may lift the fog of confusion or indecision and allow the light of truth to shine through. For instance . . . if a discussion of faith versus feelings seems appropriate or necessary, you may wish to use an illustration such as one of the following:

Picture three people stepping into an elevator. All want to go up to the seventh floor. One is laughing, another is crying, the third is unemotional. They push the button for the seventh floor, and the doors close.

How many of them arrive? Obviously, all three. Their feelings did not matter. What mattered was that they trusted the elevator to get them to the seventh floor, and they committed themselves to it. It carried them to the seventh floor, regardless of what they felt or didn't feel.

When people come to Christ, some may laugh, others may cry, and some may not feel anything in particular. What matters is that they put their trust in Jesus to get them to heaven. They commit themselves to Him—feelings or no feelings—and He guarantees to get them there. Faith is the root, feeling is the fruit, of trusting Christ.

I have another favorite illustration that I have used successfully many times as I've witnessed. In a clear and unmistakable way, it illustrates the folly of trying to be "good enough" to merit salvation.

Suppose there are two horses in a very barren field. Adjacent to their field is a very lush green pasture full of delicious, tasty grass. It looks like heaven to those two hungry horses. They gallop up to the entrance where there is a huge sign: For Sheep Only. Now, one of these horses is gentle and good. Everyone says so. Children can safely ride him, he never bucks and he delicately takes lumps of sugar from their little hands. He never kicks. He never runs away. He patiently allows himself to be saddled and ridden. He is a good horse. The other horse, however, is a mess. He is incorrigible—biting, bucking, and kicking everything and everybody within reach.

Which one of these horses will be allowed in the sheep pasture? Neither, of course. It doesn't make the slightest difference if one is good and one is bad. They have the wrong nature! They would have to be born again, become sheep by an act of God, in order to enter the sheep pasture. So it is with all men, "good" or "bad," by man's standards. Heaven is for God's sheep only. No one can go to Heaven until they become God's sheep by the new birth.

Let's add another element to the animal story. Suppose a pig tried to become a sheep by acting like a sheep. What then? Imagine that the pig was clothed in sheep's wool. He eats sheep feed, and slowly, laboriously, even learns to bleat like a sheep (in a piggy sort of way). Wherever sheep gather, he gathers. Would that change the pig's nature and make him a sheep? Would it make any difference whether the pig was "good" or "bad" by pig standards?

Of course not. So it is with trying to act like a Christian in order to become a Christian. It's impossible! It takes a miracle, the new birth. Just as it would take a miracle from God, a new birth, for a pig to become a sheep, so it takes a miracle from God, the new birth, for a sinner to become a child of God, a Christian (see John 1:12; 3:3). These two simple stories graphically illustrate these verses, and also illustrate Luke 18:10–14, where the "good" man remained lost, and the "bad" man, the repentant sinner, found salvation!

The next illustration is dynamite to any individual's claims of being good or keeping the commandments to obtain eternal life. No one can get to heaven by good works, but through Jesus alone!

The Ten Commandments are like ten links in a chain. James 2:10 declares, "For whoever shall keep the whole law, and yet stumble in one point, he is guilty of all." Suppose a man was hanging over a cliff by a ten-link chain. How many links would have to be broken before he fell to his death? No one ever has or ever can keep all of the Ten Commandments. For this reason, we are held guilty of breaking them all. All men are lost, and our only hope is Jesus. Go, my friend, and tell the story.

Other Books by Floyd C. McElveen

McElveen has over 1.1 million books in print, with 360,000 copies in Russia of "Evidence You Never Knew Existed" that is also published in Russia as "The Compelling Christ," but most often under the title of "Facts You Need to Know About."

This book is published by the thousands in China in Simplified Chinese and Mandarin, and in Korea. It has also been translated and published in Romania. Pastors are using the English version for outreach and discipleship, ordering and distributing hundreds of copies of this small but powerful book in their communities and to their people for outreach.

With the Bible League projects now complete, McElveen's books are in 8 or 9 languages. He recently wrote a book, published by Huntington Press, "The Disney Boycott." It is clear, concise, and gets to the heart of the real issue regarding the homosexual lifestyle being promoted by Disney.

McElveen's latest book published by Big Mac Publishers is perhaps the crowning jewel, "So Send I You," (previously as "Unashamed, A Burning Passion to Share the Gospel,") which was endorsed by Dr. John Ankerberg, Dr. John Morris, the late Jerry Falwell and others.

Other books McElveen has written include, "The Beautiful Side Of Death," "The Mormon Illusion," currently published by Kregel, and "God's Word, Final, Infallible and Forever," published by Gospel Truth Ministries, "Faith of an Atheist," published by Big Mac Publishers, and "The Call of Alaska," published by Promise Publishers. This book was subsidy-published, financed by Rocky McElveen, one of my sons.

For those interested in "Evidence You Never Knew Existed," the book can be ordered individually or in bulk from Gospel Truth Ministries, Fax 616-451-8907, or Ph. 616-451-4562, or Gospel Truth Ministries, 1340 Monroe Avenue, N.W., Grand Rapids, Michigan 49505.

Recently, McElveen has written a book, and acted as producer of "Jesus Christ-Joseph Smith, a Search for the Truth," in a DVD, with over 500,000 now distributed in English and thousands more translated into Spanish. The DVD is based on the book, so both have the same title.

Any effort not glorifying God is futile, but we pray and believe God has led us, in this republished version.

Pastor/Missionary Floyd McElveen
and his beautiful wife, Virginia.

If this book has been a blessing to you, encouraged you or helped motivate you to be a soul-winner, please share with us. If you have questions, please contact Mac or Virginia McElveen, by email: mac4christ@comcast.net or snail mail: 16 Sweet Bay Trail, Petal, Ms. 39465 or phone: 1-601-584-7123.

www.ingramcontent.com/pod-product-compliance
Lightning Source LLC
Chambersburg PA
CBHW020507030426
42337CB00011B/273